EXPERIENCING RUSH

The Listener's Companion
Gregg Akkerman, Series Editor

Titles in **The Listener's Companion** provide readers with a deeper understanding of key musical genres and the work of major artists and composers. Aimed at nonspecialists, each volume explains in clear and accessible language how to listen to works from particular artists, composers, and genres. Looking at both the context in which the music first appeared and has since been heard, authors explore with readers the environments in which key musical works were written and performed.

Experiencing Jazz: A Listener's Companion, by Michael Stephans
Experiencing Led Zeppelin: A Listener's Companion, by Gregg Akkerman
Experiencing Mozart: A Listener's Companion, by David Schroeder
Experiencing Rush: A Listener's Companion, by Durrell Bowman
Experiencing Stravinsky: A Listener's Companion, by Robin Maconie
Experiencing Verdi: A Listener's Companion, by Donald Sanders

EXPERIENCING RUSH

A Listener's Companion

Durrell Bowman

ROWMAN & LITTLEFIELD
Lanham • Boulder • New York • London

Published by Rowman & Littlefield
A wholly owned subsidiary of The Rowman & Littlefield Publishing Group,
Inc.
4501 Forbes Boulevard, Suite 200, Lanham, Maryland 20706
www.rowman.com

16 Carlisle Street, London W1D 3BT, United Kingdom

British Library Cataloguing in Publication Information Available

Library of Congress Cataloging-in-Publication Data

Bowman, Durrell.
Experiencing Rush : a listener's companion / Durrell Bowman.
pages cm. – (The listener's companion)
Includes bibliographical references and index.
ISBN 978-1-4422-3130-6 (cloth : alk. paper) – ISBN 978-1-4422-3131-3 (ebook)
1. Rush (Musical group)–Criticism and interpretation. 2. Rock music–History and criticism. I.
Title.
ML421.R87B69 2015
782.42166092'2–dc23
2014020879

∞ ™ The paper used in this publication meets the minimum requirements of
American National Standard for Information Sciences Permanence of Paper
for Printed Library Materials, ANSI/NISO Z39.48-1992.

Printed in the United States of America

To my parents, Lorne and Elaine Bowman, who enabled my earliest experiences of music and helped me out during some of my leaner periods along the way.

CONTENTS

SERIES EDITOR'S FOREWORD

The goal of the *Listener's Companion* series is to give readers a deeper understanding of pivotal musical genres and the creative work of their iconic practitioners. Contributors meet this objective in a manner that does not require extensive music training or any sort of elitist shoulder rubbing. Authors of the series are asked to situate readers in the listening environments in which the music under consideration has been or still can be heard. Within these environments, authors examine the historical context in which this music appeared, exploring compositional character and societal elements of the work. By positioning the reader in real or imagined environments of the music's creation, performance, and reception, readers can experience a deeper enjoyment and appreciation of the work. Authors, often drawing on their own expertise as performers and scholars, are like tour guides walking readers through major musical genres and the achievements of artists within those genres, replaying the music for them, if you will, as a *lived* listening experience.

In so many ways, Rush should not have succeeded as a rock band. Since the release of its first album in 1974, only one of its songs ("Tom Sawyer") has ever received serious radio airplay. In the early 1970s, it ignored the trend of writing anthemic hippie rock. By the late 1970s, it showed no interest whatsoever in dabbling in disco like the Rolling Stones or Rod Stewart. Nor did it don makeup and adopt glam-inspired pseudonyms, apropos David Bowie or, more outrageously, KISS. As the 1980s ushered in the era of MTV, Rush refused to package its music in postapocalyptic videos featuring leggy dancers and poor choreography. No reports ever circulated of band members being arrested at airports or sleeping with age-inappropriate supermodels. Rush never pandered to supposed working-man music fans with simple riffs and even simpler lyrics. And in the digital age, there are no phone-captured rants of drunken band members mucking about onstage. Breaking so many rules onstage, offstage, and in the recording studio, what made these guys so popular?

Perhaps breaking all these rules did it. Personally speaking, Rush is one of my top three rock bands, and as such, I feel more than qualified to answer the above question from the admittedly irrational point of view of a fan who can only shout: "Because they're awesome!" Seriously, however, what Rush accomplished was remarkable: in brief, it found a niche between the cracks of what all other rock bands had to offer, developing a taste for those in-between states among a loyal fan base; no other band could fully satisfy the needs fans never even knew they had. The music of Rush is not "beautiful" in any conventional sense. I, like any listener, remain continuously impressed by the beauty of the unique musical craft of the three virtuoso musicians who comprised the band. If anything, their utter respect for the music they created, the brand they represented, and the legacy they left behind for other musicians seeking inspiration are themselves sources of inspiration. Through the decades of performing and recording, and despite the critical neglect—Rush never won a Grammy—the band maintained a bedrock sense of reality leavened by self-effacing humor. Guitarist Alex Lifeson's "blah-blah" acceptance speech at the Rock and Roll Hall of Fame exemplifies the Dadaistic perfection of Rush that most ego-driven rock royalty could learn a little something from.

The music of Rush is best explained by a fan of the music with years of perspective and academic training, someone well capable of identifying the idioms of the band over the course of its long career. With a doctorate from UCLA and years of published writings on Rush, Dr. Durrell Bowman is exactly the right person to take up the challenge of explaining the myriad complexities and shifting sensibilities of this unique forty-plus-year act. *Experiencing Rush* successfully navigates difficult waters, offering, in my view, a far more eloquent way of saying, "They're awesome."

Gregg Akkerman

TIMELINE

August 1968	First performances by Rush (Alex Lifeson, John Rutsey, and Jeff Jones); Geddy Lee replaces Jones
January 1969	Lindy Young joins Rush
May 1969	Lee leaves Rush and forms Ogilvie, which is then renamed Judd; Joe Perna replaces Lee in Rush, and Rush is renamed Hadrian; Young joins Judd, and Hadrian disbands
September 1969	Lee, Lifeson, and Rutsey re-form as Rush
February 1971	Mitchell Bossi joins Rush for a few months (until May 1971)
1973	Rush single: "Not Fade Away" (Buddy Holly) and "You Can't Fight It"; debut album *Rush* recorded between early 1973 and November 1973
February 4, 1974 to January 31, 1975	Tour of Canada and the U.S. in support of *Rush*
March 1, 1974	*Rush* released in Canada by Moon Records
Spring 1974	Rush signed by Mercury Records
Summer 1974	*Rush* rereleased by Mercury Records
July 29, 1974	Neil Peart replaces Rutsey

February 14 to July 29, 1975	Tour of the U.S. and Canada in support of *Fly by Night*
February 15, 1975	*Fly by Night* released
March 24, 1975	Juno Award for Most Promising Group of the Year
August 24, 1975 to February 21, 1976	Tour of the U.S. and Canada in support of *Caress of Steel*
September 24, 1975	*Caress of Steel* released
March 2 to August 1, 1976	Tour of the U.S. and Canada in support of *2112*
April 1, 1976	*2112* released
August 7, 1976 to June 13, 1977	Tour of the U.S., Canada, and Europe in support of *All the World's a Stage*
September 29, 1976	*All the World's a Stage* (live) released
May 1977	Anthem Records founded (to co-release Rush's albums in Canada)
August 17, 1977 to April 8, 1978	Tour of the U.S., Canada, and Europe in support of *A Farewell to Kings*
September 1, 1977	*A Farewell to Kings* released by Mercury/Anthem
March 28, 1978	Juno Award for Group of the Year
April 1978	*Archives* (boxed set of *Rush*, *Fly by Night*, and *Caress of Steel*) released
May 10–20, 1978	Mini-tour of the U.S. in support of *Archives*
1978	*Rush through Time* (European compilation of 1975–1977 tracks) released
October 14, 1978 to June 4, 1979	Tour of the U.S., Canada, and Europe in support of *Hemispheres*
October 29, 1978	*Hemispheres* released
March 21, 1979	Juno Award for Group of the Year
August 17 to September 22, 1979	Warm-up mini-tour of the U.S., Canada, and Europe

January 1, 1980	*Permanent Waves* released
January 17 to June 22, 1980	Tour of the U.S., Canada, and Europe in support of *Permanent Waves*
September 11 to October 1, 1980	Warm-up mini-tour of the U.S.
February 12, 1981	*Moving Pictures* released
February 17 to July 5, 1981	Tour of the U.S. and Canada in support of *Moving Pictures*
October 29, 1981	*Exit . . . Stage Left* (live) released
October 29 to December 22, 1981	Tour of Europe and the U.S. in support of *Exit . . . Stage Left*
April 1–14, 1982	Warm-up mini-tour of the U.S.
September 3, 1982 to May 25, 1983	Tour of the U.S., Canada, and Europe in support of *Signals*
September 9, 1982	*Signals* released
September 18–23, 1983	Warm-up shows at Radio City Music Hall in New York, N.Y.
April 12, 1984	*Grace under Pressure* released
May 7 to November 25, 1984	Tour of the U.S., Canada, and Japan in support of *Grace under Pressure*
March 10–15, 1985	Warm-up shows in Florida
October 29, 1985	*Power Windows* released
December 4, 1985 to May 26, 1986	Tour of the U.S. and Canada in support of *Power Windows*
September 8, 1987	*Hold Your Fire* released
October 29, 1987 to May 5, 1988	Tour of the U.S., Canada, and Europe in support of *Hold Your Fire*
January 10, 1989	*A Show of Hands* (live) released
1989	Rush signs with Atlantic Records
November 21, 1989	*Presto* released by Atlantic/Anthem
February 15 to June 29, 1990	Tour of the U.S. and Canada in support of *Presto*

March 18, 1990	Juno Award for Artist of the Decade (1980s)
September 4, 1990	*Chronicles* (compilation) released by Mercury/Anthem
March 3, 1991	Juno Award for Best Hard Rock/Metal Album—*Presto*
September 3, 1991	*Roll the Bones* released by Atlantic/Anthem
October 25, 1991 to June 28, 1992	Tour of the U.S., Canada, and Europe in support of *Roll the Bones*
March 29, 1992	Juno Award for Hard Rock Album of the Year—*Roll the Bones*
October 19, 1993	*Counterparts* released
January 22 to May 7, 1994	Tour of the U.S. and Canada in support of *Counterparts*
September 10, 1996	*Test for Echo* released
October 19 to December 18, 1996	First tour (of the U.S., plus Toronto) in support of *Test for Echo*
May 6, 1997	*Retrospective I (1974–1980)* (compilation) released by Mercury/Anthem
May 7 to July 4, 1997	Second tour (of the U.S. and Canada) in support of *Test for Echo*
June 3, 1997	*Retrospective II (1981–1987)* (compilation) released by Mercury/Anthem
November 19, 1998	*Different Stages* (live) released by Atlantic/Anthem
May 14, 2002	*Vapor Trails* released
June 28 to November 23, 2002	Tour of the U.S., Canada, Brazil, and Mexico City in support of *Vapor Trails*
February 11, 2003	*The Spirit of Radio: Greatest Hits 1974–1987* (compilation) released by Mercury
October 21, 2003	*Rush in Rio* (live) released by Atlantic/Anthem
April 4, 2004	Juno Award for Music DVD of the Year—*Rush in Rio*

May 26 to October 1, 2004	Tour of the U.S., Canada, and Europe in support of *Feedback*
June 29, 2004	*Feedback* (tribute EP) released
November 22, 2005	*R30: 30th Anniversary World Tour* (live) released
April 25, 2006	*Gold* (compilation) released by Mercury
June 13, 2006	*Grace under Pressure Tour* (1984, live) released by Mercury/Anthem
May 1, 2007	*Snakes & Arrows* released by Atlantic
June 13 to October 29, 2007	Tour of the U.S., Canada, and Europe in support of *Snakes & Arrows*
April 11 to July 24, 2008	Tour of the U.S., Puerto Rico, and Canada in support of *Snakes & Arrows Live*
April 15, 2008	*Snakes & Arrows Live* (live) released
March 3, 2009	*Retrospective III (1989–2008)* (compilation) released
November 17, 2009	*Working Men* (live compilation) released
March 30, 2010	*Time Stand Still: The Collection* (European compilation) released by Universal
June 29 to October 17, 2010	Tour of the U.S., Canada, Brazil, Argentina, and Chile ("Time Machine" Tour)
August 31, 2010	*Icon* (single-disc compilation) released by Universal
March 27, 2011	Juno Award for Music DVD of the Year—*Rush: Beyond the Lighted Stage*
March 30 to July 2, 2011	Tour of the U.S., Canada, and Europe ("Time Machine" Tour, part 2)
July 19, 2011	*Icon* (double-disc compilation) released by Universal
November 8, 2011	*Time Machine 2011: Live in Cleveland* (live) released by Roadrunner/Anthem
June 12, 2012	*Clockwork Angels* released by Roadrunner/Anthem

September 7 to December 2, 2012	First tour (of the U.S. and Canada) in support of *Clockwork Angels*
April 18, 2013	Rush inducted into the Rock and Roll Hall of Fame
April 18 to August 4, 2013	Second tour (of the U.S., Canada, and Europe) in support of *Clockwork Angels*
April 21, 2013	Juno Award for Rock Album of the Year—*Clockwork Angels*
September 20, 2013	*Vapor Trails Remixed* released by Atlantic/Rhino
September 27, 2013	*The Studio Albums 1989–2007* (7-CD and 7-LP boxed set) released by Rhino
November 19, 2013	*Clockwork Angels Live* released by Roadrunner/Anthem
June 12, 2014	The members of Rush receive honorary Doctorate of Music degrees from Nipissing University in North Bay, Ontario.

INTRODUCTION

Why Rush?

Before the show in a crowded arena, a man in his thirties spots an old friend and yells across to him: "Dude—I totally knew you'd be here! It's been a really long time." They introduce their wives, exchange a few pleasantries, and return to their assigned seats. In their teens, these men bonded musically, but afterward they moved on—into careers and long-term relationships and on to new friends. They live in the same city but have not kept in touch during the several thousand days since high school. Similar white males in their twenties, thirties, and forties comprise about two-thirds of the audience for the music about to be heard. However, the audience also includes people of African descent, Asians, Latinos, indigenous persons, women, teenagers, small groups, couples, and families. How can the audience simultaneously be so specific and so varied? It's because musicians of various types appreciate the music's complexity, while their friends and others can still enjoy its accessibility.

Unexpectedly, the stage includes a row of several clothes dryers, into which a roadie feeds quarters over the next several hours and out of which the band eventually throws freshly laundered (i.e., *not* band sweat drenched) T-shirts into the audience. The dryers also participate in a humorous video component—referencing clothes dryers as black holes (presumably for socks)—that accompanies an otherwise deadly serious science-fiction song during the band's encore. As the band prepares to take the stage at the beginning of the show, the visual effects crew dims the lights almost completely and a brief musical prelude features a recording of the Three Stooges' jaunty theme song—itself a variation on "Three Blind Mice." (The band about to play consists of three members.) The concert-event thus provides a sense of awe in tension with a subtle sense of humor, and the band's music similarly inscribes various tensions.

The band's songs derive from several decades, careening among hard rock's emotive riffs and solos, heavy metal's power and intensity, and progressive rock's structural and metrical complexities. However, the band also sometimes employs stylistic fragments of the blues, rhythm and blues, jazz, jazz-rock fusion, reggae, funk, rap, classical, world, folk, post-punk, new wave, synth pop, and alternative rock types of music. Jazz appears most overtly in the drum solo, which includes swing band video components, and the bassist-singer and guitarist follow this by performing an acoustic, folklike, "unplugged" version of one of the band's songs. The band uses the same set list and song details tonight as it does for all the performances in this five-month concert tour. Moreover, apart from a handful of preplanned variations, it performs the songs in nearly the same form as when it originally composed and recorded them. Much of the audience sings along, but a large number of them also "play along" on air guitar, air bass, air keyboards, and, especially, air drums. For these fans, especially the many musician-fans, the prescribed form of the concert provides more than just something to enjoy. This evening's music—by the Canadian progressive hard rock band Rush—gives these fans something to believe in.

In the "post-counterculture," certain types of music have appealed to a large fan base that believes in such things as technique, professionalism, technology, and entrepreneurialism. Rock critics and others usually preferred reactive/revolutionary music, but musician-fans and others from the postindustrial working and lower-middle classes often preferred adaptive/evolutionary music. The latter group welcomed rock music that explored unusually mathematical time signatures, complex song forms, and instrumental virtuosity within the rhetorical service of science fiction, adventure, and a wide variety of comparably serious topics. This type of music included a successful series of albums and concert tours of "musicians' music" by Toronto-based Rush (see alsohttp://www.rush.com). The band's music features Geddy Lee's virtuosic bass playing and countertenor singing, Alex Lifeson's precise-yet-tuneful guitar playing, and Neil Peart's elaborately constructed drumming and lyrics. The band's "middlebrow" fans revered it for pursuing an eccentric and individual path over several decades, for subverting expectations about the music industry, and, as one musician-fan suggested, for "teach[ing] musicians to grow and improve themselves."

Rush would not have developed an eccentric "progressive hard" style without the example of eclectic, "musicianly," British, progressive rock from 1969 to 1974: groups such as Yes, King Crimson, and early Genesis. However, the band's music also relates to the influence of eclectic, blues-oriented hard rock and power-oriented proto-heavy metal from the same period, such as by the British groups Cream, Led Zeppelin, and the Who. On the one hand, Rush peaked commercially in the first half of the 1980s, with its only U.S. Top 40 hit in 1982 (i.e., the No. 21 "New World Man," from *Signals*) and its four new studio albums from 1981 to 1985 almost immediately certified as platinum (i.e., U.S. sales of over one million). On the other hand, Rush never functioned as a "one-hit wonder" (a phenomenon otherwise very common in the early 1980s), because the band sold considerably more copies of its earlier albums (1974–1981) in the decades well *after* its only U.S. Top 40 hit.

Rush quickly built an extensive nonmainstream audience by playing an especially large number of concerts in the mid- to late 1970s, growing from performances as an opening act to occasionally headlining in smaller venues to consistently headlining in major venues within the three years from 1974 to 1977. In its career up to 2014, Rush had sold about forty-five million albums and fifteen million concert tickets. Cities in which the band played the most frequently across its many full-length tours from 1974 to 2006 (averaging sixty-five shows per tour) included Detroit, Philadelphia, Los Angeles, San Francisco, St. Louis, Dallas, New York, Boston, Chicago, and Toronto. Album-oriented rock radio stations that supported Rush included Cleveland's WMMS (100.7), Los Angeles's KLOS (95.5), Houston's KLOL (101), Toronto's Q107, and Edmonton's 100.3 "The Bear." Many such stations differentiated their programming from former Top 40 music as "classic rock that *really* rocks."

Rush has primarily been successful in the United States (75 percent of the band's market) and its native Canada (12.5 percent, despite having only one-tenth the population of the United States), plus smaller markets in the UK, Germany, Japan, and Brazil (about 3 percent each). Based on music collection patterns and concert attendance figures for the band's fans, there are probably at least one million hard-core Rush fans worldwide, plus an additional two million or so relatively serious, secondary fans. Musician-fans comprise about two-thirds of Rush's hard-core fans. Although white males make up many of them, the figure of two-thirds musician-fans holds across *all* categories of hard-core Rush fans, such as males, females, whites, nonwhites, working class, middle class, in their forties, and in their teens. These musician-fans include a variety of amateur musicians and professional musicians, such as professional U.S., Canadian, UK, and other rock musicians from the 1970s–2000s, plus classical string musicians, jazz musicians, and others. The context is one of mainly Anglo-American rock musician–fans (plus their friends and relatives) within a technique- and differentiation-oriented, postindustrial post-counterculture.

In July of 2003, Rush played a selection of 1977–1991 album rock songs in front of 490,000 rock music fans at a post-SARS megaconcert in its hometown: "Molson Canadian Rocks for Toronto." The ten-hour event also featured the Rolling Stones and AC/DC (who played last and second last, just after Rush); Rush's fellow Canadians the Guess Who and Blue Rodeo; shorter sets by Canadians Katherine Edwards, La Chicane, Sass Jordan, Sam Roberts, and the Tea Party; with U.S. artists the Flaming Lips, the Isley Brothers, and Justin Timberlake; and a Blues Brothers revival called the Have Love Will Travel Revue, fronted by Canadian comedian Dan Aykroyd and U.S. comedian Jim Belushi (brother of original Blues Brother John Belushi). Even the Rolling Stones had never played an event with an audience this large. Rush began with its best-known song, "Tom Sawyer" (1981). Later, the band introduced its performance of "The Spirit of Radio" (1980) with an instrumental rendition of the Rolling Stones' "Paint It Black" (1966). I noticed that many concertgoers, who were overwhelmingly fans of artists other than Rush, appreciated the band's "progressive rock" musicianship, interplay, and complexity, but I also noticed that only a few people in this large, general audience knew enough of the band's lyrics to sing along with most of its songs. By comparison, most people—including a surprising number of teenagers—knew many of the lyrics of the classic rock songs—that is, classic *Top 40* rock songs—performed by AC/DC and the Rolling Stones. (Younger concertgoers were probably introduced to such music by their parents.) On the other hand, tens of thousands of Rush fans probably also attended the concert.

Within its ongoing progressive hard rock framework, Rush has explored a variety of types of music. The band synthesized them into something new that still made sense as Rush. It continued to do so over several decades, and that served to reinforce the band's pedagogical status among its hard-core musician-fans. The band's "permanent change" retained certain tendencies, such as individualism, literary lyrics, and instrumental virtuosity. On the other hand, the band also engaged with other musical styles (e.g., post-punk, synth pop, and alternative rock) and other lyrical themes (e.g., relationships and the environment). Rush's lyrics provide important meanings in most of the band's songs, and lyricist-drummer Neil Peart has been influenced by numerous books and authors—but with a particular interest in twentieth-century fiction, such as by Bellow, Capote, Delaney, Hemingway, Kerouac, London, Rand, and Tolkien. However, Rush's music reveals at least as much as their lyrics. The band often explores ideologically revealing instrumental sections. In particular, it commonly introduces textural, metrical, rhythmic, tonal, tempo, and/or dynamic changes to address things otherwise avoided musically and lyrically in the same song.

In addition to its nineteen studio and nine live albums, over its career Rush released an album of tribute songs, eleven compilation albums, ten video collections (often of live concerts), seventy-eight singles, two retrospective live tour albums (from 1984 and 1974), a remixed album, and thirty-two music videos for specific songs. The band's biggest year was probably 1981. In that year, Rush received more U.S. platinum certifications than for any other artist in the world: for its earlier breakthrough studio album: *2112* (1976), for its first live album: *All the World's a Stage* (1976), and for its recent, very successful album: *Moving Pictures* (1981). From 1980 to 1985, Rush's five new studio albums and one live album all went U.S. platinum. Between 1981 and 1995, the RIAA (Recording Industry Association of America) upgraded the certifications of Rush's four U.S. gold albums of the 1970s (five hundred thousand copies each) to at least single platinum status, and by 1993–1995 it had certified Rush's four previously uncertified albums of the 1970s as U.S. gold. The RIAA also recertified several post-1970s Rush albums at higher levels. Rush's U.S.-certification levels place the band third—behind only the Beatles and the Rolling Stones—for the most gold or platinum albums by a rock band. The band won numerous awards in its native Canada from the mid-1970s through the 1980s, 1990s, and 2000s. Its individual members also won many reader-based accolades in U.S., Canadian, and other musicians' magazines across the same decades. However, Rush's international success and influence within a broader—and arguably more mainstream—context was then eventually recognized more fully in the 2000s. It culminated with the band's induction in 2013 into the U.S.-based Rock and Roll Hall of Fame.

As you read the book, please listen to the music being discussed and/or view relevant images and videos. Rush's music can be purchased almost anywhere recordings are sold, such as via Apple's iTunes Store and at Amazon. However, you can also find the band's songs and videos by going to YouTube and searching "rush band" or for the name of a particular song or album. Note that YouTube includes numerous cover versions of Rush's music (such as by fans and tribute bands), as well as many live versions by Rush of its own songs. So, searching simultaneously for the band name plus album and/or song name will narrow your results considerably, such as "rush hold your fire." Many results include fan-provided images or lyrics, so also adding the words "original" and/or "video" can help narrow things further, such as "rush counterparts stick it out original video." In some cases, a Rush song title also provides the name of an album, so adding the word "album" or "song" would help clarify things, such as "rush clockwork angels original song." In addition, the band's lyrics can be found on any number of websites, such as LyricsMode (see http://www.lyricsmode.com/lyrics/r/rush). To find relevant Rush-related images, you could go to Google Images and search "rush band." To see an album cover, search on the band and album name simultaneously, such as "rush moving pictures."

I

"FINDING MY WAY"

From Blues Rock to Arty Hard Rock, 1968–1975

Rush formed in Toronto in the late summer of 1968 and included fourteen- to fifteen-year-old guitarist Alex Lifeson (b. Aleksandar Živojinović; August 27, 1953, Fernie, British Columbia), his neighbor and schoolmate, drummer John Rutsey (b. May 14, 1953, Toronto, Ontario; d. May 11, 2008), and bassist-singer Jeff Jones (b. September 20, 1953, Chicago, Illinois; later a band member of Canada's Red Rider with Tom Cochrane). The band name "Rush" certainly implies "adrenaline rush" or "drug rush." The term refers most directly to a substance commonly sold as "video head cleaner" but used illegally as an inhalant narcotic: butyl nitrite. Throughout the 1970s, the members of Rush became increasingly involved in their family lives. Thus, they said very little about the band name's origin, occasionally deflected it as a generic word, and, unlike journalists, avoided using the word for obvious punning. Guitarist turned bassist-singer Geddy Lee (b. Gary Lee Weinrib; July 29, 1953, Toronto, ON) replaced Jeff Jones in September of 1968, and multi-instrumentalist and singer Lindy Young (Lee's eventual brother-in-law) also temporarily joined the band around Christmas of that year. In early 1969, Lee left Rush and formed Judd (initially called Ogilvie), and Rush was renamed Hadrian. Young then joined Judd, but by the fall of 1969 Judd had also disbanded, and Lifeson, Rutsey, and Lee reformed as Rush.

WEEKEND WARRIORS: EARLY RUSH, 1968–1974

In the earliest years of Rush, the band mostly played cover versions of well-known rock-and-roll and rock songs, initially by Cream (e.g., blues-rock), then Jimi Hendrix's "Fire," the Rolling Stones' "Satisfaction," Them's "Gloria," Buffalo Springfield's "For What It's Worth," John Mayall's "You Don't Love Me," and also songs by Elvis Presley, the Who, Traffic, Ten Years After, and Willie Dixon. Rush re-formed in 1969 with fellow Toronto teenager Ray Danniels as the band's manager. The band picked up on the eclecticism, high vocals, and distorted electric guitar of the newly formed UK rock band Led Zeppelin. By 1971, Rush played mostly original songs in this vein, and in that year it briefly experimented, once again, with adding a fourth member (second guitarist Mitchell Bossi). The Ontario government lowered the drinking age from twenty-one to eighteen in the spring of 1971 (it later raised it to nineteen), and the band could soon play in bars, including Toronto's Gasworks and Abbey Road Pub, instead of mainly at coffeehouses, high school dances, and outdoor recreational events.

Geddy Lee says of the band's late-sixties/early-seventies origins:

> We were very typically suburban: What you'd call [a] "weekend warriors" kind of thing. We were growing our hair, and . . . "in that club of rebels," I guess is the best way to describe it. . . . [We] longed to break out of the boring surrounding of the suburbs and the endless similarities . . . the shopping plazas and all that stuff. . . . [The] music . . . was a vehicle for us to speak out. (*In the Studio with Redbeard* 1989)

The aspect of "escaping from suburbia" alluded to by Lee suggests that even working-class, high school dropouts could exemplify the post-countercultural aesthetic of staking one's claim to a rewarding life and career. Musicians of this type almost always began their careers as "weekend warriors"—that is, playing rock music on weekends in order to escape from conventional jobs held on weekdays. However, some of them eventually had the opportunity to pursue professional ambitions through recording contracts and concert tours. The success of Rush and others inspired numerous fans in their teens and early twenties to pursue their own goals and develop their own ideals. Indeed, the subject matter and musical content of various old and new Rush songs spoke to these concerns as subsequent generations of young fans entered the workforce.

On specific early influences on his bass playing, Lee says:

> I was first influenced by [Cream] bassist Jack Bruce. Cream was one of the groups that I loved when I was growing up and first got into music in a more serious way. We used to play Cream songs way back when. What I liked about Jack was that his sound was distinctive—it wasn't boring, and it wasn't typical. And he was very busy. . . . He was obtrusive, which I like in a bass player. (Tolleson 1988)

By "busy" and "obtrusive," Lee refers to playing notes and passages that do more than merely reinforce the bass notes of a chord progression. Cream-influenced—and post-Cream—rock music resonated for tens of millions of rock fans and millions of aspiring rock musicians in the 1970s, 1980s, and beyond.

In discussing Rush's stylistic origins, Lee explains: "I guess in the beginning, we were just a straightforward rock band. We grew out of things like Led Zeppelin, Jeff Beck, and bands like that" ("Interview with Geddy Lee" 1978). Lee doesn't really mean that Led Zeppelin's or Jeff Beck's music is straightforward, because it isn't. Rather, he means that guitar-based, blues-influenced hard rock covers what hundreds of thousands of rock musicians aspired to at the time. By 1970–1971, Alex Lifeson played power chords (carefully tuned, distorted open fourths or fifths) and blues rock electric guitar riffs, largely inspired by Led Zeppelin's Jimmy Page. Geddy Lee sang in a high vocal style, largely inspired by Led Zeppelin's Robert Plant, but "countertenor"—falsetto based, though very resonant; rather than Plant's high, comparatively natural, powerful tenor. Rush's first full-length concerts of mainly original songs took place in Toronto and Detroit in early 1972. In 1973, Rush attempted a hit single cover version of Buddy Holly's 1957 rock-and-roll classic "Not Fade Away," with an original song, "You Can't Fight It," on the B-side. The single introduced Geddy Lee's still-immature use of his high, piercing vocal style, but it was rather ill suited to Holly's pop-rock song. The single flopped, but around that time the cash-impoverished band also opened concerts at Toronto's Victory Burlesque Theatre for the proto-punk/glam band the New York Dolls.

RUSH (1974)

In 1973, Rush booked off-peak recording studio time to make a full-length album for a total cost of $9,000. Rush's eventual (1974–1982) coproducer Terry Brown, a UK expatriate (nicknamed "Broon") who had earlier worked with a number of well-known groups in the UK (e.g., the Who, Donovan, the Troggs, and Procol Harum), helped the band complete the album. In the process, they judiciously discarded "Not Fade Away" and "You Can't Fight It." Moon Records (run by Ray Danniels and Vic Wilson) independently released the self-titled album *Rush* in Canada in March of 1974. The original, Canadian front cover showed an explosion, with "RUSH" spelled out in large, bright red letters. It was designed by Paul Weldon. The album combines the style of Led Zeppelin's acoustic/electric rock eclecticism with boogie/blues hard rock, the latter more in the style of such younger U.S. bands as Aerosmith and KISS.

"Finding My Way," the album's opening song, deals with a man pursuing a woman even though she ended their relationship when he went on the "road." It served as a last-minute replacement for Rush's commercially unsuccessful cover version of Buddy Holly's "Not Fade Away." The second song, "Need Some Love," concerns (not surprisingly, given its title) the sexual pursuit of a member of the opposite sex. "Take a Friend" (third) concerns the desirability of close platonic friendships. "Here Again" (fourth) takes its cue from the slower, more mystical and dynamically varied side of Led Zeppelin (e.g., "Dazed and Confused" and "Thank You"). In it, the band seems much more introspective and soul searching.

The album's fifth song, "What You're Doing," opens its second half. It presents, in heavy metal style, an angry tirade, possibly against people who might have preferred that the band pursue a more commercial sound. The circa 1971 song, "In the Mood" (sixth), and—after its multi-guitar instrumental introduction—"Before and After" (seventh) also recall the recall the relationship-based subject matter and riff-based style of Aerosmith, KISS, and Led Zeppelin (e.g., "Communication Breakdown" and "Heartbreaker"). Aerosmith and KISS both also released debut albums in 1973–1974 and both provided Rush with opening-act opportunities around 1974–1975. On all but one song on the album

(Lee's "In the Mood"), bassist-singer Geddy Lee and guitarist Alex Lifeson are both credited with the music and the lyrics.

"Working Man"

The best-known song from Rush's debut album is "Working Man" (eighth and last, 7:09). The band wrote the song in 1971, several years before it turned professional. The song appealed to the continuing, suburban working class, as well as to members of the emerging, postindustrial class, including people in their late teens. It lyrically concerns the activities of a working-class male. He gets up at seven, puts in a full workday, and returns home and enjoys a beer, but doesn't readily accept the situation of being stuck in such a daily routine. He complains about not having "time for living" and dreams about someday being able to live a better life.

The song's music suggests influences from early Cream and Led Zeppelin blues rock. Instrumentally, such groups usually made use of electric guitar, electric bass, and drums, and they also had significant guitar-solo components. Like Cream, Rush is a "power trio," where an instrumentalist (e.g., the bass player) is also a singer. Geddy Lee's unusual, often-high, countertenor singing style spans around three octaves, from baritone through tenor, alto, and mezzo-soprano pitch ranges. Typical for Rush's early music, "Working Man" has a lot of instrumentals and guitar solos, no keyboards or other electronics, no backing vocals, and uses a straightforward, common-time, 4/4 time signature. The song mainly uses a slow, "walking" pace, even though most of Rush's other songs are at faster tempos.

The song uses a powerful, two-bar (two-"measure"), electric-guitar riff (first at 0:00–0:12) that is somewhat similar to those created by British band Black Sabbath. The song is thus arguably an example of "heavy metal." The riff leaps positively from the song's main pitch to one just shy of an octave higher. It then falls dejectedly through a third, midpoint pitch on its way back down to the starting note. The second measure leaps to a different midpoint note, this time "snaps" actively upward to the riff's highest note (the top note of the original leap), but again falls back to the starting note. The two-measure unit then begins again, still trying to rise up or escape, but always falling back to the same place. The riff thus means being stuck somewhere, such as in a working-class job. The riff also underlies the song's verses (initially at 0:12–0:37), and Lee's vocal melody similarly uses only a few notes: "I get up at seven. . . . I'm working all the time. . . ."

The song's brief chorus is sung over a different, "taunting" riff (originally at 0:37–0:46). The notes of that riff are faster and move impatiently back and forth across open intervals. Lee repeats the verse's last line (the "tag": "They call me the working man"), and the music again attempts to escape to a more positive sound. The chorus concludes, though, with: "I guess that's what I am." Lee's vocal melody ends up on a quite low note, and the song's original, main riff also returns (0:46–0:58). Both elements mean that the working man is stuck in his situation. Verse 2 (0:58–1:22) lyrically has to do with the end of a workday, grabbing a beer, and pessimistically complaining about "nothing going down here." After a repeat of the song's chorus (1:22–1:31), Alex Lifeson this time contributes a bluesy, emotive guitar solo (1:31–1:55) over the resumed, main riff. The chorus then reappears (1:55–2:04), followed by a brief, bass-guitar interlude (2:04–2:10).

Alex Lifeson's more lengthy, second guitar solo (starting at 2:10) twice breaks out into a fast, multi-instrument, unison "middle" section (at 3:13–3:32 and 4:34–5:00). The solo appears over a syncopated rhythm that evokes a 1950s rhythm and blues pattern often associated with the African American musician Bo Diddley. (A similar pattern is used in Buddy Holly's "Not Fade Away," which Rush covered in 1973.) The second solo, the syncopated rhythm, and the unison middle sections are considerably more active and positive sounding than the rest of the song, and they also make up nearly half of it. Eventually, though, the song's pessimistic aesthetic returns, in its main, slow riff (at 5:18–5:30), a reprise of verse 1 (at 5:30–5:54), and the chorus (at 5:54–6:15). Toward the song's ending (at 6:15–6:39), the band makes its already-slow, main riff even slower. Bent-pitch "groans" (at 6:39–6:54) and full-band solidarity with them (at 6:54–7:10, the end of the song) further enact the song's frustration.

"Working Man" is semiautobiographical. The band members dropped out of high school around 1968–1969, and for the next several years they mostly did working-class jobs: working in a convenience store, assisting a plumber, changing flat tires, pumping gas, and house painting. Similarly, the band's eventual permanent drummer-lyricist— Neil Peart (pronounced "Peert," b. September 12, 1952, Hamilton, Ontario) sold trinkets to tourists while otherwise attempting to establish a music career in England around 1970–1972. Afterward, he played drums part-time in Ontario (ca. 1972–1974, e.g., in the cover band Hush), while working at the farm implement shop where his father worked. At the time of writing this song, the members of Rush were still struggling in such working-class jobs.

The escape from one's employment situation ultimately proves impossible in "Working Man," and you may have once felt—or feel now—that way yourself. Later Rush songs (1975–2012) also resonated for its hard-core and casual fans. The band's fans are around 78 percent male and 22 percent female, 90 percent white, generally started listening to the band's music in their late teens, were by the 1990s or 2000s typically in their thirties or forties; 80 percent had at least some kind of postsecondary training; and around 70 percent were at some point active at least as amateur musicians (Bowman 2003). Rush later explored a lot of different types of music and lyrical themes, but it never covered the working-class territory of "Working Man" again. On the other hand, the song does appear on Rush anthologies, in cover versions (e.g., even providing the title of *Working Man: A Tribute to Rush*, various artists, 1996), and so on.

TURNING PROFESSIONAL

Import copies of Rush's self-titled debut album made it to Cleveland, Ohio's flagship rock radio station (WMMS, 100.7 FM) in the spring of 1974. Station programmer Donna Halper championed it (especially "Working Man"), and the band suddenly had a much larger audience. The similarity of "Working Man" to a number of Led Zeppelin songs also worked in Rush's favor in the summer and fall of 1974, and Donna Halper suggests that some Cleveland area listeners thought "Working Man" actually *was* by Led Zeppelin (Banasiewicz 1988, 14). Part of the confusion came from Led Zeppelin being in between album projects in 1974.

Rush started to play as an opening act at important rock shows, partly via U.S. booking agency ATI. Cliff Burnstein of the U.S. label Mercury Records signed the band to an album deal and re-released the debut album in the United States. Rush almost signed with Casablanca

Records, which had just released KISS's debut album but later became known mainly for disco and other dance-pop music. The Mercury version of *Rush* reproduced the original album cover, except that a technical error turned the word "RUSH" into pink instead of the original red. Around the same time, original drummer John Rutsey suddenly quit the band. He cited differences in musical direction (i.e., a continuing interest mainly in blues rock) and his health (he was a diabetic) as an explanation. In the summer of 1974, just before the band's first major tour (often opening for KISS), St. Catharines, Ontario, native Neil Peart replaced Rutsey.

During the fall of 1974, Rush appeared on a number of live/radio simulcasts and television shows, including *The King Biscuit Flower Hour, Don Kirshner's Rock Concert*, ABC's *In Concert*, and the Toronto show *Boogie*. For example, on the Kirshner show the band played "Best I Can" (by Lee, later recorded for Rush's second album, *Fly by Night*) and "In the Mood" and "Finding My Way" from *Rush*. By the end of the band's first tour, *Rush* had sold seventy-five thousand copies in the United States. The band became increasingly well known in the United States for its subsequent albums, songs, and music videos. It also toured extensively in the States over several decades. However, after 1975 Rush did not again appear "live" on a U.S. TV show until *The Colbert Report* in 2008. The band enjoyed a somewhat higher media profile in Canada, though, and in 1975 it won the Juno Award ("Canadian Grammy") for Most Promising Group of the Year.

In the 1970s, '80s, and beyond, industrial, manual laborers transformed into technicians, clerks, customer service representatives, secretaries, administrative assistants, courier-drivers, and hundreds of thousands of amateur musicians. Rush's combination of a strong work ethic and libertarianism appealed to many such people. In the same period, as office employees transformed into lawyers, teachers, architects, social workers, engineers, consultants, administrators, computer programmers, and hundreds of thousands of additional musicians, Rush's entrepreneurial values and individualism appealed to many others. Hundreds of thousands of hard-core fans in both groups found Rush's music sublimely and quintessentially post-countercultural.

Geddy Lee once spoke of Rush's early music as a kind of prehistory:

I can't [listen] back beyond *2112* [1976] really. . . . If I hear "Lake-side Park" [from *Caress of Steel*, 1975] on the radio, I cringe. What a lousy song! Still, I don't regret anything that I've done! (Johnson 1993)

On the other hand, the band still occasionally played a few songs written between 1971 and early 1975 (especially "Working Man") during its live shows in the 1980s, 1990s, 2000s, and 2010s.

By late 1974, though, Rush's new drummer-lyricist, Neil Peart, began to take some of Rush's lyrics into a more literary direction. Concurrently, on its second and third albums, the band began to combine the power-based aspects of heavy metal with bluesy hard rock and certain metrical and structural complexities from progressive rock.

FLY BY NIGHT (1975) AND TOWARD PROGRESSIVE ROCK

Rush recorded its second album, *Fly by Night* (1975), with the band's new drummer-lyricist Neil Peart in ten days at Toronto Sound in January of 1975. The album cover greatly improves on the album cover of *Rush*. It features a painting by Eraldo Carugati of a bright-eyed bird of prey spreading its wings above a snowy landscape. The band coproduced the album with Terry Brown, who had helped complete Rush's debut album in 1973.

Many people equate progressive rock with psychedelic rock, but they are very different genres, with very different types of complexities. Progressive rock features predetermined, though often extended, "album-oriented" music, and it is reproduced in almost exactly the same way *even* when it is performed live—such as by Yes, Rush, or Dream Theater. It is thus somewhat analogous to—even arguably a replacement for—certain types of classical music. By comparison, psychedelic rock features improvised, often extended, "jam band" music, *especially* when it is performed live—such as by the Doors, the Grateful Dead, or Phish. It is thus somewhat analogous to certain types of jazz. The audience for the two types of music did, however, overlap.

Progressive rock appealed mainly to white males, but it also resonated for certain female and nonwhite musician-fans and for the emerging, postindustrial community of workers. Even though such fans considered this music to be on a higher plane than commercial popular music, some 1970s progressive rock bands became at least as commercially successful as many pop groups. For example, Pink Floyd, Genesis, Yes, Emerson, Lake & Palmer, and Jethro Tull each sold several million copies of at least several different albums. Various features of progressive rock appealed to an audience that admired complexity and construction at least as much as spontaneity and soul. In addition to time signatures, this approach involved large-scale formal design and intricate microstructures.

"Anthem"

Fly by Night's opening song, "Anthem" (credited to all three members, 4:26), indicates Rush's emerging fascination with rhythmic complexities. In its introduction (0:00–0:33) the song immediately presents material in the irregular time signature of 7/8. The first (or "top") number of a time signature represents the number of beats per measure (or "bar"), and the second (or "bottom") number specifies the duration of each of those notes. Thus, 7/8 means seven counts each lasting an eighth note. The most common time signature is 4/4: four beats each lasting a quarter note. Most rock songs in irregular time signatures (such as in 5/4 or 7/4) drop or add one quarter note per measure. For example, the verse section of the Beatles' "All You Need Is Love" (1967) sounds like it lacks the last quarter note of every other measure. Pink Floyd's "Money" (from *Dark Side of the Moon*, 1973) sounds like the musicians add an extra beat for every two measures of 3/4. Peter Gabriel's "Solsbury Hill," from his self-titled debut (1977), cleverly masks a 7/4 time signature in the service of an allegory about the freedom of having escaped from the "machinery" of his former progressive rock band, Genesis. In the opposite direction—the *non*-masking of "odd" meters—a number of early-1970s UK progressive rock bands (e.g., Emerson, Lake & Palmer, Yes, Genesis, Gentle Giant, and Jethro Tull) explored the possibility of subdividing time signatures at much faster tempos and with briefer durational note values. For example, they used 7/8, 13/8, 15/16, and other asymmetrical constructions in alternation with more common ones. Such elements required skills in mathematics, in addition to considerable performance virtuosity and technique.

The opening, 7/8 section of Rush's "Anthem" also largely distills the band's interest in unison instrumental sections into the song's opening thirty-three seconds. The song's introduction accomplishes several things. First, it complicates Rush's emerging, eclectic hard rock style by introducing elements characteristic of UK progressive rock. Second, it establishes drummer-lyricist Neil Peart as an equal participant in the band's musical-social collaboration. Third, the song introduces what would eventually become Rush's signature rhythm: 7/8 arranged as 2+2+3.

The band wrote certain aspects of "Anthem" during Neil Peart's band audition in late July of 1974, which probably suggests that Lee and Lifeson already wanted to move in this direction, whereas the band's original drummer did not. Although Peart could also play with a power matched by very few rock drummers, some of his contributions to this early Rush song include a high degree of virtuosity. In most of Rush's music, Peart played with the butt end of his drumsticks flat across an unusually large portion of his drumheads. This enabled considerably louder and fuller sounds than he could achieve by playing with the tip ends of his sticks.

"Anthem" also established a post-countercultural model for individualism, with words about "living for yourself," finding "new wonders," and so on. The band must have intended the song as a harbinger ("anthem") of its "progressive hard rock" direction, and verse 1 (0:53–1:07) encourages listeners to "keep on looking forward." The lyrics' selfishness motif and the coinciding verse/chorus music—anxiously paced, in a major key—suggest a brash swagger, and Lee's extremely high vocals (averaging nearly an octave above middle C) amplify its intensity. Lifeson's emphatic, anticipated major-chord riff introduces all three verses (0:33–0:53, 1:23–1:36, and 3:09–3:23), and into the verses themselves Lee's vocal gestures contradict Peart's backbeat snare.

The song title "Anthem" and certain elements of the song's lyrics invoke the "virtue of selfishness" espoused by Russian-born American author Ayn Rand. The quip in the song's lyrics about "bleeding hearts" suggests that lyricist Neil Peart dislikes—or disliked—liberalism, but in interviews and elsewhere he also indicates a dislike for conservatism. Most critics heard Rush's stylistic and lyrical elements as arrogant and self-absorbed. However, the band's fans heard the same features as liberating and instructive: a trio of hardworking, ambitious, twenty-two-year-old high school dropouts from Canada figured out how to make a unique place for themselves in the highly mediated world of rock music. Harmonically, "Anthem" is quite complex, with pitch alternatives making possible some unexpected key relationships and unusual chord progressions. It amounts to quite a lot of ambivalence about the irrational nature of a not very accommodating society.

The Rest of *Fly by Night*

Some of the album's songs recall the eclectic hard rock and boogie-blues of the band's first album, but others introduce new elements. Geddy Lee's "Best I Can" (second) recalls the earlier riff rock and antiestablishment posturing of the band's earlier song "What You're Doing." Lifeson and Peart's "Beneath, Between & Behind" (third) embodies a relatively heavy hard rock style and lyrically begins to show Peart's predilection for social critique. The song touches on the irony of transplanted nobility having to contend with waves of working-class immigrants and continental expansionism in the aftermath of the American Revolution. The words "Ten score years ago, defeat the kingly foe" refer to the approaching U.S. bicentennial. "By-Tor & the Snow Dog" (8:39) credited to all three members and placed fourth, anthropomorphizes two fighting dogs as medieval knights, one evil (the "By-Tor" or "biter") and the other virtuous (the "Snow Dog"). It depicts the dogs' growling battle instrumentally (with bass fuzztone/phaser effects and guitar whammy/vibrato effects) and lasts for more than nine minutes. It also somewhat connects to the subject matter of Rush's later song "The Necromancer" (*Caress of Steel*, also 1975).

Lee and Peart's title song, "Fly by Night" (placed fifth) opens the album's second half. It features pop-like hooks and a pleasant, moderately fast tempo, but it also shifts among different rhythms within musical phrases. The song became an album-oriented rock (AOR) radio staple. Although it never charted as a U.S. Top 40 hit, it also opens the anthology *'70s Greatest Rock Hits, Volume 1* (Priority, 1991). "Making Memories" (sixth), credited to all three members, recalls Led Zeppelin songs based around short, "snappy" guitar riffs (and slide technique), such as "Ramble On" and "Gallows Pole." Lee and Peart's "Rivendell" (seventh) gently evokes J. R. R. Tolkien's (1892–1973) Middle-earth homeland of the immortal elves, a haven of safety and healing for travelers in *The Lord of the Rings* (1954–1955). Thus, the song mirrors the fascination for Rush and their Anglo-American fans with UK fantasy literature. Lee and Lifeson's "In the End" (the eighth and final song) recalls the slow blues of the band's earlier song "Here Again," as well as such Led Zeppelin songs as "Babe I'm Gonna Leave You" and "Since I've Been Loving You." With the exception of a few intentionally dropped beats (and the progressive rock–inspired beginning of "Anthem"), Rush's first two albums use relatively conventional rhythms and time signatures.

CARESS OF STEEL (1975)

Rush's third album, *Caress of Steel* (1975), credits all three band members with the words and music, but Peart probably wrote most of the lyrics. Peart's studio-effected voice speaks the introduction of "The Necromancer." Lifeson uses a rented Fender pedal steel guitar for part of the song. He also rented a Fender Stratocaster for "Lakeside Park" and borrowed a classical guitar for the "Panacea" section of "The Fountain of Lamneth." The album cover—the first of several dozen by Rush associate, fellow Canadian, and occasional guest keyboardist Hugh Syme—includes a Tolkien-like fantasy painting (a man standing on a misty mountaintop, a pyramid, a snake) and a foldout design. Syme's intended metallic color scheme (to reflect the "steel" of the title) became a more muted, copperish hue at the printer. The band recorded the album at Toronto Sound in July of 1975, coproducing it with Terry Brown.

"Bastille Day"

The album's opening song, "Bastille Day" (4:40), exemplifies the type of relatively short song that the band successfully interspersed among its more extended and conceptual fare in the same period. As with "Working Man" and "Anthem," "Bastille Day" uses a heavy metal or hard rock style (again without keyboards or acoustic guitar) to argue its ideological viewpoint. Like "Working Man," it makes use of powerful chords, 4/4 time, and "four-square" phrases. However, it also features complex, busy rhythms and frequent chord changes. The band uses these elements much more prominently in this song than in "Working Man" or in the postintroduction sections of "Anthem."

As with the 7/8 opening of "Anthem," Lifeson begins this song with an introductory guitar riff *not* later reprised in the song. The riff announces, as with a fanfare or a film studio motto, a new beginning at the start of this album (0:00–0:17). The song's main, six-note guitar riff (first presented in repetition at 0:17–0:36) then features an energetic, anticipatory rhythm. It rises four times: twice by leap, then by step, and then by leap again. As in many hard rock songs, this main riff introduces and then underscores the song's verses. Although the pitches here recall those in the main riff of "Working Man," the faster tempo (112 vs. 78 beats per minute) suggests a much more frantic context, and the several rhythmic anticipations also give a powerful sense of urgency. Unlike the world-weary insistence on a returning, low pitch in the earlier song's main riff, the same pitch here functions merely as a starting point. Moreover, the riff's consistent upward motion gives a sense of "rising," which perfectly suits the song's modernist/Enlightenment lyrics about the inevitability of political democracy.

The first two verses (0:36–0:45 and 1:15–1:25) outline the sympathetic viewpoints of various observer-participants of the late eighteenth-century French Revolution. On the other hand, the riff's fast tempo and frantic nature also risk falling apart musically. Also, the lyrics of chorus 1 and 2 (0:45–1:05 and 1:25–1:45, not set to the song's main riff) contradict its otherwise sustained use of a certain, positive-sounding harmonic shift. These choruses suggest that even democracy can go awry, and they subtly change in grammatical meaning as the song proceeds, from third-person plural to first-person plural: from "They're marching to Bastille Day" to "We're marching to Bastille Day." Verse 1's "Let them eat cake" quotes Marie Antoinette's famously out-of-touch quip about the masses, and the "bloody prize" refers to the head of Louis XVI. Although the Bastille-storming of the French Revolution took place four years before the comparative nastiness of the king's beheading, the album title (*Caress of Steel*) presumably refers to the gruesome functioning of a guillotine.

An extended instrumental section (starting at 1:45) follows chorus 2, continuing the song's relatively positive turn, including a kind of "jazz-rock" guitar solo (1:55–2:15). After thirty seconds, a contrasting, active, middle section (2:15–2:48) adds guitar-solo elements and sequentially rising patterns. These precipitate a shift in the sentiments of the lyrics into the third (and final) intro-verse-chorus segment (2:48–3:23). Verse 3 and chorus 3 also involve democracy in the Western world, but are now generalized to refer to the "present" (the mid-1970s). In the post-counterculture, "anger burns" because a corrupt, new nobility flaunts its wealth and power. History has taught its lessons, and money buys more than just power. Here, Peart may mean corporations and/or the music industry. His distaste for "soulless" wealth and power along those lines later surfaced in a number of Rush songs. However, in the particular context of this early song, Rush wanted to insist on doing things its own way: morality despite freedom; individualism within democracy; libertarianism as guillotine.

The song's chorus is comparatively optimistic (in a major key), provides a marchlike texture, is solidified harmonically, and becomes increasingly active rhythmically. However, it also finds its way back to the song's original, more ambivalent, minor key. Also, in chorus 3 (at 3:23–4:05) the band reworks some of its earlier instrumental music. However, this time the material is made consistently frantic sounding, unison textured, and excludes any elements of the former guitar solo. This provides a powerful sense of a band of ideologically like-minded— though perhaps also confused—individuals uniting for a guillotine-like cause.

"Bastille Day" ends with a half-speed, reflective, hymnlike, instrumental version of the chorus (4:05–4:36). It preserves optimism, however, by remaining in the song's major-key alternative until the very end of the song. This contemplative ending drives home the band's point that even democracy can lead to unpleasantness (as in the aftermath of the French Revolution) and that individuals wishing to succeed within capitalism are usually not sufficiently strong-willed to avoid the tyranny of corporate greed.

The Rest of Caress of Steel

"I Think I'm Going Bald" (the album's second song) uses a hard rock, boogie blues style to inscribe the semihumorous, self-deprecating subject matter of its lyrics. It may also be Rush's silliest song. The pop-hook-inflected song "Lakeside Park" (third) was influenced by rhythm and blues and lyrically addresses hometown nostalgia and the lost innocence of one's teenage years. These topics resonated for many Rush listeners. Neil Peart named the song after an actual park in his hometown of St. Catharines, Ontario, and it also references fireworks on the "24th of May"— which is the traditional date for Canada's Victoria Day holiday. As with the title track of *Fly by Night*, record companies sometimes included the song on anthologies of 1970s rock. The album ends with two, extended, multimovement, sword-and-sorcery suites: "The Necromancer" (12:32 and related to "By-Tor & the Snow Dog" on the previous album) and "The Fountain of Lamneth" (19:57). They take up nearly three-quarters of the album, thus providing further evidence of Rush's interest in "serious" aspects of UK progressive rock. However, as with the working-class elements of "Working Man," Rush's initial foray into fairly obvious sword-and-sorcery elements was short lived.

Around 1975, Rush had an especially "1970s" look, with long hair, Lifeson's bare chest, Peart's prominent mustache, Lee's bell-bottom trousers, and so on. The band generally wrote material for its following album while on tour, such as during free time when its members would have otherwise just been sitting around in hotel rooms. Lifeson most often played a Gibson ES-335 (Electric Spanish) guitar, Peart played Slingerland drums and Zildjian cymbals, and Lee usually played a Rickenbacker 4001 bass. The 1975–1976 concert tour for *Caress of Steel* was not very successful, and the band nicknamed it the "Down the Tubes" Tour. Not surprisingly, Rush's U.S. record company wanted them to pursue a more commercial direction. However, instead of agreeing to become *more* mainstream sounding and *less* serious in 1976, the band at first spent several years becoming *less* mainstream sounding and *more* serious. The band pursued the correct path for itself, though. Its audience grew considerably larger from later 1976 to 1981, and the band quickly established itself as a large-scale touring act internationally. Several decades later, almost all rock bands that had been more commercial sounding in the 1970s and '80s (e.g., with Top 40 hits and even No. 1 pop hits, such as Journey and Foreigner) mostly played in relatively small, "nostalgia" venues. Rush, though, remained a major album and touring act for several decades and continued to fly in the face of mainstream-music and record-company expectations.

2

"THEIR OWN MUSIC"

Progressive Heavy Metal, 1976–1977

Certain works on Rush's 1975–1981 albums applied large-scale musical/formal design to pursue individualism and other topics relevant to the post-counterculture. The band's first significant breakthrough along those lines came with the science-fiction-oriented album, *2112*, but the more philosophical album, *A Farewell to Kings*, is artistically at least as successful.

2112 (1976)

2112 is mostly known for its musically complex, stylistically aggressive, and ideologically confusing, opening title-suite. The band again recorded in Toronto and coproduced its music with Terry Brown. The album was certified as U.S. gold (five hundred thousand copies) in 1977, platinum (a million copies) in 1981, and triple platinum (three million copies) in 1995. A deluxe edition of the album with bonus live tracks and updated packaging was released, not surprisingly, in 2012.

"2112" (The Song)

Rush's first extended work of the late 1970s—"2112" (with a duration of 20:33)—explores a rather extreme form of individualism. Neil Peart's lyrics slightly evoke the influence of the novella *Anthem* (1938) by Russian-born American writer and philosopher Ayn Rand (1905–1982). That book had already appeared in Rush's music as the title of one of its earliest songs involving Peart. "2112," though, is much more despairing than Rand's novella and, in fact, also much less like Rand's self-oriented, Objectivist philosophy than Rush's earlier song "Anthem." Indeed, it is much more similar to George Orwell's bleak, dystopian, 1949 novel *Nineteen Eighty-Four*. In addition, the band uses varied styles, alternating textures, specific gestures, and contrasting tonal areas to explore its philosophical theme *musically* in a way that would not have made sense to Rand. In essence, "2112" is about a lot more than just its general, partial lyrical similarities to the text of Rand's book. It is also the band's first, very strong fusion of progressive rock with hard rock and heavy metal.

Peart sets "2112" in a futuristic alien dystopia, and he pursues a proindividualist/antitotalitarian subject matter. A number of rock critics, though, associated Rush's worldview with fascism. Such commentators used "2112" and the band's general affinity for Rand's individualist philosophy and strongly willed literary characters as evidence for this interpretation. Rand's characters that fit this profile include the stubborn, antimainstream architect Howard Roarke in *The Fountainhead* (1943) and the antigovernment-regulation industrialists in *Atlas Shrugged* (1957). A more balanced interpretation of Roarke, et cetera, holds that rational/ethical egoism makes perfect sense, because it aligns one's market value to people who understand your views and thus feel an affinity for your work. The members of Rush believe that this scenario is a very good thing, but so do a lot of other people. Revealingly, Peart considers himself a "left-wing libertarian" ("A Rebel and a Drummer," *Liberty*, September 1997) by which he means that he dislikes the political right's intolerance and support of censorship and is terrified of religious fundamentalism, while at the same time recognizing that the left can be intolerant. He probably also favors a smaller, more efficient government that doesn't interfere with one's personal liberties, but that does also provide an essential "safety net" of social services, such as for the less fortunate. (The band eventually contributed considerable amounts of money to various independent agencies and causes, such as through the activities and campaigns of the United Way.)

"2112" lyrically transliterates certain postcollectivist, postactivist, and post-countercultural ideas for the rock generation of the 1970s and beyond. The *music* of "2112" also does so, but in a complex, potentially confusing way. The work inverts one of the main conventions of Western narratives: hero, conflict, resolution. Even in classical music's instrumental sonata form, for example, a melody or theme (the musical equivalent of a hero) generally establishes order, falls into conflict with a disturbing force (other tonal areas, rhythms, textures, and so on), then emphatically reestablishes itself. By comparison, in the earliest sections of "2112," Rush tells us about an assertive, administrative, priest collective that is the *antihero* of a futuristic, totalitarian star system. The actual hero is someone else, but we don't meet him right away, and he is much less assertive.

Overview of "2112" (from *2112*, 1976)
The indicated section names are provided on the album itself.

Overture (0:00–4:32)
The Temples of Syrinx (4:32–6:43)
Discovery (6:43–10:15)
Presentation (10:15–13:57)
Oracle: The Dream (13:57–15:58)
Soliloquy (15:58–18:18)
Grand Finale (18:18–20:33)

The work starts with an instrumental "Overture" (0:00–4:32). It begins with nearly a minute of mechanical sounds, including high filter sweeps and low oscillations played on an ARP Odyssey synthesizer by the band's cover artist, Hugh Syme. These sounds then merge with sputtering, distorted, and echoed bass/guitar-chord pairings, which solidify into a highly rhythmic heavy metal riff and begin to preview themes from later in the work, as in an opera overture. Performances of "2112," including versions appearing on Rush's various live albums, also include the audience yelling the syllable "hey" on recurring upbeats of certain rhythmically animated, heavy metal segments. In addition, the section incorporates a quotation from a classical music instrumental overture: Tchaikovsky's *1812 Overture* (1869).

Emerging from the Tchaikovskian battle explosions of the "Over-ture" comes Geddy Lee's natural baritone voice in a brief vocal ending (at 4:25) on the oddly Bible-referencing words: "And the meek shall inherit the earth." Given the chant-like nature of the melody and the narrative's eventual outcome (it doesn't end well for the narrative's meek "hero"), the band probably intended this quotation from Jesus's "Sermon on the Mount" as ironic. Neil Peart also sometimes uses bibli-cal imagery elsewhere in his lyrics, but doing so results from his broad-based literary and cultural influences, not from wishing to validate any particular religion. In a related matter, many rock-music-hating Chris-tians interpreted Rush's use of an image of a naked man recoiling from a red pentagram (on the back cover of *2112* and elsewhere) as satanic. However, Satanists actually position pentagrams with a single point pointing downward (not upward), not to mention that recoiling from an image means the complete opposite of endorsing its meaning. Indeed, "2112" is ultimately about an individual going up against the masses of a collectivist mentality. That idea is represented in the work musically and lyrically, but it is also indicated in the album's cover image.

In the work's second section, "The Temples of Syrinx" (4:32–6:43), the band uses the genre of heavy metal rock, Lee's high/piercing vocals, and a chorus solidly in a certain minor key to portray the collectivist priests as irrational. The small number of different sung notes and the aggressive, steady-stream nature of the section's opening verse evoke the priests' delusional pride in controlling such things as literature, music, and art. The following chorus changes the tone only slightly, with frantic rhythms (ahead of the beat) and shorter phrases giving an even better sense of their swaggering pride in their "accomplishments." The priests recall similarly unpleasant forces in the original *Star Trek* TV series (1966–1969), the science-fiction film *Logan's Run* (1976), and so on.

"Discovery" (6:43–10:15) follows. In this section, the narrative's "hero"—an individual male—learns about and explores music on his own, which is something his society does not allow. His music is gentle and exploratory, not at all like the forceful and determined attitude we normally expect from a hero. He somewhat parallels Equality 7-2521 in Rand's *Anthem*. Her hero rediscovers his individual identity, partly through rediscovering scientific principles, technology, and reinventing the electric light. In Rush's version, he experiments not with the electric light, but the electric *guitar*.

In a brief correspondence by "Anonymous" (dated 2112), the album's liner notes indicate that the man's home city is the generically named Megadon, that the planet Syrinx has twin moons, and that "the Red Star of the Solar Federation" banded the solar system's surviving planets together fifty years ago and now provides (Orwellian) Templevision and Temple Papers. Above this, the album's band photo shows Lifeson, Peart, and Lee wearing Asian-like, silken wraps above bell-bottom pants. Concert photos from this period sometimes show the band members wearing similar flowery/paisley silk vests (sometimes without shirts underneath), and Lifeson apparently sometimes wore bell-bottoms. The band members have long, 1970s-style heavy metal hair, and Peart has a thick, dark mustache.

Like Equality 7-2521, Peart's hero threatens the prescribed social order through his individual, creative activities. He experiments with the guitar, learns how to tune it, and begins to play it. He finds his way from open (unfretted) strings to related major and minor keys. To further differentiate him from the shrieking/authoritarian priests, Lee sings in a lower/"normal" baritone vocal range. The music also remains gentler and more reflective and includes the water-based sounds of falling rain and/or babbling brooks. This drastically contrasts the onslaught just encountered in the "voice" of the priest collective. Our hero can't wait to "share his new wonder," so that other people will also be encouraged to "make their own music."

In "Presentation" (10:15–13:57), our hero brings his discovery ("an ancient miracle") to the priests and attempts to convince them of its merits. Lifeson's music uses a pleasant, jazz-inflected, rhythm and blues (R&B), major-key style that was somewhat anticipated during part of the "Discovery" section. The priests, though, chastise him, because when individual music still existed, it ostensibly "helped destroy the elder race of man." They argue the guitar is a "toy" that "doesn't fit the plan." To make it clear that the priests will not tolerate individual creativity, their violent, minor-key, heavy metal music from the "Temples of Syrinx" section reappears (at 13:00). Also, the section's guitar solo has the effect of further dismissing the individual's wide-eyed optimism and, instead, underscoring the extremely negative ideological position of the priest collective.

Up until this point in the piece, "2112" may have seemed a bit like some kind of latter-day version of Timothy Leary's famous 1967 countercultural, hippie phrase: "Turn on, tune in, drop out." However, Rush's hero doesn't actually want to "drop out." He already did that (in "Discovery"), and now he wants (in "Presentation") to bring what he learned back to society. In a sense, then, it's almost the complete opposite of Leary, and if it thus inscribes a kind of "post-counterculture," then maybe it's just culture. Indeed, the "2112" scenario parallels the similar concerns about social and moral contributions expressed by working-class, early-1970s, late teens in sociological research of the 1980s. In some of that research (Victoria Anne Steinitz and Ellen Rachel Solomon, *Starting Out: Class and Community in the Lives of Working-Class Youth* [Philadelphia: Temple University Press, 1986]) informants emphasized their desire to contribute to society. Also, like Rush, they expressed a "belief in the value of hard work" and a related "respect [for] the gains of wealthy people when [seen] as individuals rather than as collaborators in the economic system" (Steinitz and Solomon 1986, 56).

In the fifth section, "Oracle: The Dream" (13:57–15:58), our hero dreams of a "strange and wondrous land" of individualists, the works of whose "gifted hands" the society actually supports. The initial post-dream moment is called "Soliloquy" (15:58–18:18), and it rises in intensity through a three-part section (16:54–18:18) that brings closure to the hero's part of the story. He recognizes that living on his planet necessitates a "cold and empty life." His despair deepens in Lifeson's angry, frustrated, blues-rock guitar solo in the section's minor key, which is the "parallel minor" of the hero's original major key. This change in style (to blues rock) and in tonality (to the parallel minor) rejects the "jazzy" optimism and major key tonality of "Discovery" and "Presentation." Indeed, according to Peart's liner notes (and unlike anything in Rand's novella), the hero commits suicide at the end of "Soliloquy." That is not, however, the end of "2112."

The work ends even *more* negatively than mere suicide and in some ways anticipates the band's strange, individualist mini-epics of 1977: "Xanadu" and "Cygnus X-1." The "Grand Finale" (18:18–20:33) reprises the totalitarian, priest-related, heavy metal style from earlier in the work. The music becomes increasingly violent, and it includes densely layered (collective) and chaotic guitar melodies that largely fit with the priests' tonal area. The work ends extremely forcefully in an unanticipated tonality: the "dominant" of the priests' material. The band pairs this abrupt, major-chord tonal shift with a rhythmic insistence on all instruments, evoking Morse code for V/Victory: short-short-short-long. That is the same rhythmic gesture used in the famous "knocking" gesture of the first movement of Beethoven's Symphony No. 5. The extremely noisy instruments also evoke the explosions of the end of the work's "Overture."

A spoken voice joins the din on the words: "Attention all planets of the Solar Federation" (three times) and "We have assumed control" (also three times). These closing vocals appear with studio effects that make them sound disembodied and multiple. The words relate vaguely to the album's liner-note "story backdrop," but the story's ending is quite unclear. It must be the case that either (1) the "elder race" (i.e., the preauthoritarian society) has returned to regain its earlier control or (2) the priest collective has ramped up its recent control. Although some Rush fans argue for the first option, to me it seems unlikely, because Peart abhors authoritarianism. If the elder race is wise (on Peart's terms, anyhow), it would not "assume control." Also, if it is about to return, why would our hero kill himself? Thus, the second option seems by far more likely, with the priests annihilating individualist expressions recently inspired by the example of the work's hero.

Rock music scholar Deena Weinstein (1991) reports from her informal Rush fan ticket-line survey respondents, that more than 70 percent believed Rush identifies with the authoritarian priests of "2112." She often used "2112" as a case study in her course on social theory. Revealingly, she reverted to lyrics only once the confusion of the priests having the "heaviest" music became apparent. The lyrics—but *especially* the music—of "2112" expand the libertarian, individualist agenda already touched upon in earlier Rush songs. The composition also demonstrates Rush's fusion of hard rock's power with progressive rock's structural complexity. Ultimately, though, it is not much like Rand's *Anthem*.

At the end of *Anthem*, Equality 7-2521 and his beloved "Golden One" (Liberty 5-3000, the latter decidedly absent in "2112") scheme to dismantle the dystopia. By comparison, "2112" veers into a pessimistic, UK-inspired ending consistent both with John's self-flagellation, final rejection of Lenina, and suicide at the end of Aldous Huxley's *Brave New World* (1932), and with Winston's ultimate rejection of Julia and reabsorption into the Party at the end of George Orwell's *Nineteen Eighty-Four* . Musically, the layered, priest-related guitar elements in the penultimate section of Rush's "Grand Finale," the simultaneous rhythmic insistence (in all instruments) on a priest-affirming chord, and the multiple/plural "we" voice of the final "control" proclamation resoundingly defeat the antiauthoritarian/guitar-discovering hero. "2112" encapsulates the post-countercultural desire of young people wishing to contribute to society on individualist—not collectivist—terms.

In "2112," Rush "undercoded" its meanings: listeners receive only a very general sense of what is going on and thus may not correctly interpret the intended meaning. For example, popular music scholar Reebee Garofalo mentions Rush twice in his widely read 1997 textbook *Rockin' Out: Popular Music in the USA* and suggests that Rush made a "considered nod toward fascism . . . with *2112*" (1997, 292). However, that assertion is completely unfounded, as Rush and Rand are both actually *anti*fascist. Rand left early Soviet Russia for the United States in 1926 and was one of the twentieth century's most staunch advocates of individual rights and freedoms. However, it is also true that she and Rush do not demonstrate their preference for individualism in quite the same way. Peart acknowledges that the similarity between *Anthem* and "2112" was accidental:

> It ended up being quite similar to a book called *Anthem* by the writer Ayn Rand. But I didn't realize that while I was working on it, and then eventually as the story came together, the parallels became obvious to me and I thought, "Oh gee, I don't want to be a plagiarist here." So I did give credit to her writings in the liner notes. (Kordosh 1981, 62)

It was definitely a bad idea for Peart to have made "acknowledgment to the genius of Ayn Rand." Rand would never have considered "2112" (especially "Soliloquy" and "Grand Finale") as a parallel to *Anthem*, anyhow, and Peart's mention of her opened up a "can of worms" that kept Rush's work associated with her in the minds of many people—despite hundreds of further examples to the contrary. Lots of people (especially young adults) have read Rand's novels, been inspired by her strong-willed/individualist characters, and then moved on. Very few of them, however, have been rock stars.

The Second Half of *2112*

Most of the five short songs on the second half of *2112* are at least loosely and generally consistent with its opening title track. "A Passage to Bangkok" espouses access to recreational drugs in exotic lands in Latin America, northern Africa, and Asia. "The Twilight Zone" provides an homage to Rod Serling, the TV science-fiction genius who had recently died of cancer. (Rush dedicated its previous album, *Caress of Steel*, to Serling.) The song includes whispered background voices, anticipating the introduction of the *Crucible*-inspired "Witch Hunt" (*Moving Pictures*, 1981). Lifeson's "Lessons," a snappy/acoustic song about growing up (but with electric power chords in the chorus), recalls Led Zeppelin. Lee's "Tears," a mellow/semisweet song about allowing oneself to fall in love, features the distinctive, sustained tones of a Mellotron 400 keyboard, played (again) by the band's cover artist and occasional studio-album keyboardist Hugh Syme. The band designated "Tears" as the album's studio-only production song. The album's closing song, "Something for Nothing," uses a succinct, hard rock (arguably heavy metal) style to argue for a strong work ethic.

PROGRESSIVE HARD ROCK

Between 1974 and 1976 Rush's musical style changed from something rock critics could appreciate as being related to the musically adventurous side of the blues rock tradition (e.g., Cream, Led Zeppelin, and Bad Company) to a kind of bastardization involving elements of progressive rock. In a U.S. magazine review of mid-1970s Canadian rock music, Bart Testa states:

> Rush's *2112* is a rock-opera equivalent to [the science-fiction film] *Logan's Run*, and about as interesting. Rush don't exactly play rock 'n' roll anymore, which may be wise after the slapdash heavy metal of *They* [sic] *Fly By Night*. Rather, they inflict rock-like spasms to punctuate Geddy Lee's mewling recitations of his [sic] ponderous Ayn Rand sci-fi prose. . . . *2112* is still just lousy reruns of third-rate David Bowie. (1976, 73)

Testa makes numerous, basic, factual errors in his "review," but around the same time some UK (and a few Canadian) reviewers sympathized with Rush's "Anglo" leanings toward album/concert-oriented progressive rock. For example, Chris Welch points out:

> [Rush produces] concert rock of the highest calibre, involving a sophisticated light show, extended arrangements, epic lyric-writing. . . . Undoubtedly, Rush are Anglophiles . . . but [they] have a unique flavour about them, working wonders with what might be considered an exhausted vein, the three-piece guitar band. . . . [T]hey don't just blast forth, attempting to cajole audiences with brute strength, but employ a lot of subtle, spacey effects, and fully understand the need for dynamics. (1977, 38)

However, even reviews of Rush in the United Kingdom varied considerably. Writers at the *New Musical Express* definitely preferred supposedly "anticommercial" music (e.g., punk and post-punk rock—and reggae) and relatively obscure, experimental music. Rush, though, broke through to a very large audience between 1976 and 1981, and its concert tours were critical for that growth. These included performances at numerous large-scale arenas, auditoriums, and amphitheaters in the United States and Canada (nearly every year from 1974 to 2013); also at music halls in the UK and continental Europe (on many tours, from 1977 to 2013), plus music-hall and arena concerts in Japan (1984); and stadium shows in Brazil and Mexico (2002), Puerto Rico (2008), and Brazil and Chile (2010). The band's first of many live albums, *All the World's a Stage* (1976, recorded at Toronto's Massey Hall), includes a performance of most of "2112." (The band borrowed the title of the album from Shakespeare's *As You Like It*.) Most, later Rush live albums and concert videos were recorded in other countries, although many of the band's studio albums were recorded (at least in part) in Canada.

The original, 1970s understanding of "progressive rock" involved long and/or complex, composed (not improvised) songs, album-rock and concert contexts, and most often British bands. Rush's two most musically progressive studio albums are *A Farewell to Kings* (1977) and *Hemispheres* (1978). Not surprisingly, they were also the first exceptions in Rush's studio albums in being recorded in the UK instead of in Canada. Despite the fact that 1976–1979 was arguably the peak of both the disco (dance-pop) and punk rock eras, there was nonetheless considerable interest among music fans in Rush's peculiar type of progressive hard rock music.

The diversity in Rush's audience is reflected in the band's sometimes more pop-oriented—and non-British—opening acts from 1976 to 1977. Such groups included the Irish band Thin Lizzy ("The Boys Are Back in Town," 1976), the U.S. progressive-influenced pop-rock group Styx ("Come Sail Away," 1977), the U.S. pop-rock band Cheap Trick ("I Want You to Want Me," 1977), Australian hard rock band AC/DC ("Let There Be Rock," 1977), and the eccentric, Canadian pop-rock band Max Webster ("Diamonds Diamonds," 1977). Similarly, in 1976–1977 Rush itself still sometimes served as an opening act for major U.S. (especially) and British acts, including Aerosmith, Blue Öyster Cult, Kansas, Lynyrd Skynyrd, Ted Nugent, and Electric Light Orchestra (ELO). Rush became exclusively a headlining act in 1978.

A FAREWELL TO KINGS (1977)

In May 1977, Rush founded Anthem Records (later called Anthem Entertainment) as its business concern and to co-release its albums in Canada. Rush's fifth studio album—*A Farewell to Kings* (1977)—features Hugh Syme's album cover of an abandoned marionette-king splayed on a throne in front of urban decay. This evokes Rush's libertarian view of the artificiality of governments *and* religion, and it also relates to the theme of the album's opening title track. The album's back cover also reinforces this idea, by dangling the marionette's abandoned string mechanisms. The album's elaborate foldout design includes the lyrics as well as band photos by Fin Costello (both live and posed). The foldout also includes the man-and-star logo from *2112*. The band recorded the album at Rockfield Studios in Wales (coproducing it with Terry Brown) and mixed it at Advision Studios in London. In addition, Lee, Lifeson, and Peart dedicated the album to their spouses: Nancy, Charlene, and Jacqueline, respectively.

The album begins to formalize the division of labor of Rush's several previous studio albums. With only a few exceptions from 1977 to 2012, Peart received credit for Rush's lyrics, and Geddy Lee and Alex Lifeson received credit for the band's music. The opening title song, "A Farewell to Kings" (5:53), is truth and wisdom oriented and includes Life-son's classical guitar elements and Lee's Minimoog synthesizer melody. In this case, the music is credited to all three band members.

"Xanadu"

"Xanadu" (11:08), the album's "mini-epic" second track, concerns an individual, male explorer seeking paradise. (Olivia Newton-John and Electric Light Orchestra had a dance-pop movie hit of the same name in 1980, but the two songs have nothing to do with one another—lyrically or musically.) The song is 11:08 in duration and begins with several minutes of instrumental gestures that prepare in various ways for the song's second half. Some of the song's earliest guitar gestures recall the bell tower carillon melody suggestive of London's Big Ben. This gesture fits with Rush having recorded this album in the UK, with the band's decided interest in British progressive rock, and with Peart having based the song's lyrics on the poem *Kubla Khan; Or, A Vision in a Dream* (1798), by British poet Samuel Taylor Coleridge (1772–1834).

The song's lyrics feature images of a mysterious lost paradise. Despite its incomparable beauty and enveloping immortality, it ensnares its discoverer in an inescapable prison of madness. The scenario produces a lonely and bitter "triumph" for its occupant. However, such an ambivalent "resolution" is already suggested in the song's long instrumental introduction, with its sense of leaving Western civilization, battling nature, and arriving in an exotic paradise in "eastern lands unknown." The narrative also vaguely parallels the story of Orson Welles's film debut *Citizen Kane* (1941). In that movie, newspaper magnate Charles Foster Kane (portrayed by Welles) builds a magnificent mansion for himself and his second wife, a mediocre singer for whom he had also built an opera house. He names the place Xanadu—thus also referencing Coleridge—and subsequently undergoes an "ambivalence entrapment" quite similar to the one in Rush's later narrative. Coleridge's poem includes a vision of a damsel with a dulcimer. However, as with his avoidance of an *Anthem*-like female companion in "2112," Peart again avoids one in "Xanadu." The protagonist remains alone and evidently prefers it that way, which is admittedly a bit weird on an album dedicated to the band members' wives!

In the song's introduction, Lifeson plays major-key electric guitar patterns over a pedal (continuously asserted) note. These, along with accompanying bird, stream, wind, wind chime, and woodblock sounds initially evoke a lost-in-the-woods, "searching" quality. They also recall the similar elements in the "Discovery" section of "2112." In his rhythmically free guitar figurations (up to 1:49) Lifeson also explores occasional, hesitant nonchord tones as well as the provisional tonal area's second- and third-most-important chords. Later (1:49–2:52) we begin to hear his 7/8 (2+2+3) home-key rhythmic gesture, initially faded in to suggest an approach.

As Lifeson continues his insistent 7/8 pattern, his bandmates attempt to counter this with increasingly frenetic interjections on bass and drums. The present book's cover shows an image of the band performing this part of the song. The combination of Lifeson's aggressive stance and facial expression, Lee's "looser" stance and expression, and Peart's high degree of concentration exemplifies Rush's hybrid of heavy metal, hard rock, and progressive rock. Until this part of the introduction, Lee had contributed only subtle synthesizer sounds (i.e., no bass guitar) and Peart had played only gentle woodblock and wind chime sounds. (Later parts of the song get considerably more energetic sounding.) Lee and Peart's varied "objections" attempt to pull Lifeson away from his obstinate pattern (ostinato). In particular, Lee's pitches clash with Lifeson's pitches. Narratively, Lee and Peart attempt to warn Lifeson that the supposed paradise of Xanadu may end up unworthy of his obsession, but the guitarist-protagonist refuses to abandon his resolve.

In the following rollicking and syncopated 4/4 section (2:52–3:34), Peart and Lee change their tack. Their material initially seems to move somewhat closer to Lifeson's way of thinking, but Lifeson counters this by abstracting his former 7/8 obstinacy into its starkest possible form: a stubbornly repeated chord. We arrive in Xanadu through a joyous, 7/8 "real" guitar riff (3:34–4:23). Lifeson reestablishes his earlier key *and* 7/8 time signature, but both in a more complex idiom. Lee also contributes a synthesizer melody.

The band then uses a moderate tempo, extended chords, and Eastern-sounding percussion effects (4:23–4:59) to inscribe Xanadu's grandeur and exoticism. Gently syncopated, adjacent chords provide a transition to the second (sung) half of the song. The lyrics begin (verse 1, 4:59–5:15) with a carefully controlled balance in the rising versus falling of the vocal melodies, and Lee begins his vocal contributions in a relatively natural, low range. Along with gently rolling rhythms, the lyrics, such as "I will dine on honeydew and drink the milk of paradise," suggest the possibility of a lasting paradise. The instruments sound a particular pitch in all four chords that underlie this expository vocal section. The pitch arguably reflects a fulfillment of the "dominant" obsession presented earlier in the song. It also recalls the priest-affirming secondary chord at the end of "2112." However, the following transition (5:15–5:21) uses an unexpected, new, and complex tonal area to present clues concerning the true, duplicitous character of Xanadu.

The much faster chorus 1 (5:21–5:53) continues with dissonances, including a reprise of the tonality with which Lee warned against Lifeson's insistence during the earliest sections of the work. This section also incorporates a tempestuous rhythmic sense, especially compared to the gentleness of verse 1. The lyrics, in past perfect then past tense, initially provide an unsettled tone, evoking mystery, immortality, and the pursuit of paradise. Verse 2, in present infinitives and future tense, then gives a sense of being frozen in time in Xanadu. (This recalls the reverse verb tense trajectory from future to present to past in "Bastille Day.") Lee sings this in a comparatively high range, and the instruments provide a quite fast tempo as well as frantic and confused-sounding rhythms. This also contrasts with the much gentler verse 1, even though verse 2 largely reprises verse 1's words.

Xanadu's central ideological conflict concerns its combination of paradise and prison. The band explores this most fully in the song's moderate-tempo, instrumental bridge, falling between the fast chorus and slower verse. The bridge also includes a prominent, plaintively crying-out synthesizer solo (first heard at 5:53–6:15). In this section, the tonal center shifts. The band makes prominent use of a Romantic-era chord on the "flat-six" scale degree, something that often means "illusory hope." The chord reveals Xanadu as a false paradise—once there, you cannot choose to leave it. The lyrics of chorus 1 (i.e., "Time and Man alone") and the first half of verse 2 (set to the "illusory hope" chord, 6:15–6:58) portray the protagonist as the "last immortal man."

The band next inserts (at 6:58–7:39) the third portion of the instrumental introduction (originally at 2:52–3:34). It thus reprises the song's earlier, rollicking, 4/4 syncopated idiom and its joyful naiveté about arriving in paradise. However, the band this time uses this section ironically, by skipping the grandeur/exoticism portion heard earlier and plunging directly into an angry-sounding, major-key hard rock chorus (chorus 2, "A thousand years have come and gone . . . waiting for the world to end . . . ," 7:39–8:08). As before, the crying synthesizer bridge (8:08–8:31) and an "illusory hope" verse (verse 3, 8:31–9:08) follow. These modifications increase our understanding of the ambivalence experienced by the protagonist. Indeed, verse 2's "To stand within the Pleasure Dome decreed by Kubla Khan" and "To taste anew the fruits of life the last immortal man" become, in verse 3, "*Held* within the Pleasure Dome decreed by Kubla Khan" and "To taste my bitter triumph as a *mad* immortal man." Moreover, at the end of verse 3 (the song's final vocals) Lee seems to change "Oh, Paradise" into the much more ambivalent "Whoa, *is it* paradise?" The original poem contains nothing like this, and Rush's version thus ends far more ambivalently than Coleridge.

The song ends instrumentally, beginning with a reprise (at 9:08–9:32) of the obsession portion of the instrumental introduction (originally at 4:23–4:59). This evokes the optimism and grandeur/exoticism of its first incarnation (gongs, etc.). However, Lee now counters it with a very obtrusive synthesizer sound on a series of octave descents on a particular pitch. This descending gesture parallels the protagonist's insanity and reprimands him with a musical equivalent of "You asked for it!" Lifeson's reply involves a frustration-imbued solo (9:32–10:10) over the chord changes of this continuing reprise. His use of syncopated rhythms, bent pitches (via whammy bar), and frantic chromatic outbursts underscore the motif of dissatisfaction. The band uses an unsettled, unusual approach to the song's main key (10:10–10:14), just like it did earlier (at 5:15–5:21). This move confirms Xanadu as a prison and gives way to a brief reprise (at 10:14–10:27) of Lifeson's insistent 7/8 gesture. The protagonist now obsesses about *leaving* Xanadu, but he is permanently stuck there.

The song's "coda" ("tail" or ending section, 10:27–11:04) includes descending intervals on guitar in several octaves, musically characterizing the protagonist's descent into madness. The band also reprises the song's third introductory section (originally 2:52–3:34), but slows it progressively down. Peart adds somber, mysterious chime timbres to reinforce the moral of paradise's illusion. The ending thus somewhat recalls the slow, hymnlike instrumental ending of Rush's earlier "Bastille Day."

The work ends with a final "home-key" flourish that recalls the aggressive insistence at the end of "2112." However, the individual in "Xanadu" attempts to transcend society and becomes ensnared in his *own* situation.

The Rest of *A Farewell to Kings*

For "Closer to the Heart" (the album's third song, 2:54), Peart cowrote the lyrics with Peter Talbot. It is an anthem espousing diversity, was often programmed on album-rock radio stations, and remained almost continuously in the band's tour set lists for several decades. "Cinderella Man" (fourth, 4:22) has lyrics by Lee based on Frank Capra's 1936 rags-to-riches film *Mr. Deeds Goes to Town*, which starred Gary Cooper. "Madrigal" (fifth, 2:35) is a kind of love song, featuring gentle, reflective music.

All three band members also receive credit for the album's extended, closing (sixth) song: "Cygnus X-1." Like "Xanadu," it is a "mini-epic," and its full name is actually "Cygnus X-1 Book One—The Voyage." The album clarifies that the song is "to be continued." One of Rush's most musically progressive pieces, it features a substantial amount of electronically generated sounds and sound effects, frequent complexities of rhythms and time signatures, eight tonal areas, a high degree of virtuosic unison playing, and one of the smallest proportions of sung music on Rush's first five studio albums. The science-fiction song is inspired by the fact that in 1971–1972, University of Toronto astrophysicist Tom Bolton assembled solid evidence that an X-ray source—Cygnus X-1—indicates the presence of a black hole. Peart's lyrics and the band's music have to do with a solitary astronaut choosing to fly into a black hole's inescapable gravity field. "Cygnus X-1" also loosely ties *A Farewell to Kings* to the band's next album: *Hemispheres* (1978).

3

"THE UNIVERSE DIVIDED"

From Progressive Hard Rock to Post-Prog, 1978–1980

Rush has the reputation of having written a lot of long songs, and Stephen Colbert made a joke about that when the band appeared on TV's *The Colbert Report* in 2008. However, the band actually never wrote any further songs longer than seven and a half minutes after 1978, and by 1982 almost all of its new songs were about five minutes in duration. On the other hand, Rush's lengthier, progressive hard rock music did not hurt its awards recognition in its native Canada, as it won Juno Awards for Group of the Year in both 1978 and 1979. The band's most significant stylistic change took place from *Hemispheres* (1978) to *Permanent Waves* (1980).

HEMISPHERES (1978)

Rush wrote *Hemispheres* (1978) entirely in the studio, recording again in the UK, with coproducer Terry Brown. It begins with the last of the band's three, album-side-length compositions, and it also concludes with a fairly lengthy instrumental "mini-epic." Thus, it is the Rush album containing the fewest songs: four.

"Hemispheres"

Hemispheres opens with the "title" track: "Cygnus X-1 Book II Hemispheres" (18:08)—which is usually just called "Hemispheres." The full title of the final work on Rush's previous album is "Cygnus X-1 Book One—The Voyage," and it includes the added designation: "To be continued." Among other things, "Hemispheres" balances the multisectional, extended form of "The Fountain of Lamneth" (1975) and "2112" (1976) with the expanded instrumental content (e.g., synthesizers and nonstandard percussion) of the mini-epics "Xanadu" and "Cygnus X-1" (1977). The song begins with repeated statements of a jazz-influenced "extended" chord, containing a seventh and an eleventh. The same chord reappears throughout the piece, as a means of transitioning between song sections.

Lyrically, in an experiment in moving beyond the individualist narratives of 1976–1977, Peart establishes a conflict between the left (thought or "reason-oriented") and right (emotion or "feelings-oriented") halves of the human brain. He positions these halves according to classical, mythological references to the gods Apollo and Dionysus, respectively. On Hugh Syme's album cover, versions of Apollo (as a serious-looking, stiff, business-suited man, complete with bowler hat and walking stick) and Dionysus (as a naked, gesturing, "artsy"-looking figure) appear on either side of the rift between the two halves of a human brain. (See textbox below for an overview of "Hemispheres.")

> Overview of "Hemispheres" (from *Hemispheres*, 1978)
> The indicated section names are provided on the album itself.
>
> Prelude (0:00–4:29)
> Apollo—The Bringer of Wisdom (4:29–7:00)
> Dionysus—The Bringer of Love (7:00–9:06)
> Armageddon—The Battle of Heart and Mind (9:06–12:02)
> Cygnus—Bringer of Balance (12:02–17:04)
> The Sphere—A Kind of Dream (17:04–18:08)

Similar to the "Overture" of 2112, the "Prelude" (section 1, 0:00–4:29) of *Hemispheres* initiates many of the work's main musical themes in two instrumental segments (0:00–2:58 and 3:36–4:29). Some portions of the "Prelude" use unusual, complex time signatures, 7/4 and 12/8. In between the two instrumental segments, the section incorporates a vocal segment about the struggle between the gods of love and reason for supremacy over the "fate of Man" (2:58–3:36).

Next, a pair of vocal stanzas introduces "Apollo—The Bringer of Wisdom" (section 2, 4:29–7:00, ending with Lifeson's first guitar solo) and "Dionysus—The Bringer of Love" (section 3, 7:00–9:06), respectively. So as not to privilege either god, Rush gives both sides exactly the same music, much of which had already been introduced in the work's "Prelude." Apollo mentions truth, understanding, wit, wisdom, precious gifts, awareness, food, shelter, fire, grace, and comfort. Dionysus (later, to the same music) mentions love, solace, feelings, laughter, music, joy, tears, and a soothing of fears. The band highlights the opening of these sections by using its favorite, odd metrical construction: 7/8 (2+2+3). The constant motion among adjacent extended chords also underscores the instability of Apollo *and* Dionysus.

Later in each section, in rhythm and blues-inspired 4/4 music, each god encourages the people to follow his particular social plan. After instrumental interruptions recalling the work's opening, the following segments narrate (in third person) the frenetic activities of the warring and aimless people. In both cases, the people (and Rush, presumably) wonder what they lost by completely abandoning the other side. The band follows section 2 (Apollo) with Lifeson's angry-sounding, bent-pitch, heavy metal guitar solo on the same underlying 4/4 music. A gesture at the end of section 3 (Dionysus) thematically recalls gestures from the work's "Prelude."

The same "Prelude"-derived gesture is then also explored in new ways in section 4, "Armageddon—The Battle of Heart and Mind" (9:06–12:02). This section inscribes human chaos about which approach (heart/love vs. mind/wisdom) is the best way to run society. The first segment (9:06–10:57, including Lifeson's second guitar solo) uses harmonically unstable motions. During this section, the recording pans both Lifeson's solo and, later, Geddy Lee's high voice from a normal, center placement to extreme "divisions" of right and left. (Listening with headphones definitely accentuates the effect.) "Armageddon" also eventually recalls previously unreprised 12/8 music from early in the "Prelude."

The section's joyous, final 4/4 segment (10:57–12:02, initiated by a drum fill) musically and lyrically evokes a group of people who went their own way, instead of following Dionysus *or* Apollo. To musically parallel this "third option," the band uses normal, tonal music. The point of view then shifts, unexpectedly, to the astronaut from the band's earlier song, "Cygnus X-1" (1977). The individual explains that when he spiraled, in his ship (the Rocinante), into the timeless space of the black hole, he did not die. Instead, he was transformed into something else. At that point, the band reprises—from the earlier work—the semichromatic, ascending gesture that it had featured both instrumentally and vocally as the black hole took control. In "Hemispheres," Peart invents a new kind of mythology for the post-counterculture. The earlier, science-fiction song's astronaut (arguably, a kind of "martyr" for individualism) brings about the possibility of philosophically fusing heart and mind. Rush thus manages not only to enact "left-wing libertarianism," but also to espouse a relatively soulful, though usually also stylistically quite heavy, version of progressive rock.

Section 5, "Cygnus—Bringer of Balance" (12:02–17:04), initially reprises some unusual chords from the end of "Cygnus X-1." Synthesizer sounds as well as subdued "samples" from the earlier work, panned stereophonically, also take part. In this section, a "disembodied spirit" first begins to speak (12:45–14:37). Lee sings the words: "I have memory and awareness, but I have no shape or form . . ." in an almost chant-like, natural-baritone voice. Lifeson's chorused guitar effects further the disembodiment. The texture remains quite thin and the tempo slow, and the music also ebbs and flows rhythmically. Studio techniques, especially echo, also participate in this section. These effects evoke the vaguely mechanical/mystical electronic sounds that open the futuristic cityscape of Ridley Scott's later science-fiction film *Blade Runner* (1982). Lee sings about a "silent scream" building inside.

The music then explodes into a reprise of earlier music, and Lee sings very high notes again. In the work's "Prelude," struggle music (even eighth notes in 4/4) gives way to battle music (rhythmically complex, in 7/4). This time, though, the band switches these segments into the reverse order: battle (at 14:37–14:53), then struggle (at 14:53–15:24). The reversal suggests that a battle does not actually settle things, but that a different kind of "struggle" might. Apollo and Dionysus express their astonishment at the possibility of such a complex, tense balance. They had previously only conceived of having their followers choose one or the other of the "sorry hemispheres"—mind or heart. At this point, however, the two competing gods welcome him as a fellow immortal: "We will call you 'Cygnus.' The God of Balance you shall be."

Cygnus functions both lyrically and musically as a balance or compromise between Apollo and Dionysus. Lifeson's third guitar solo (15:24–15:39) also heightens this. A joyously rollicking, 12/8 hard rock "dance" (16:02–17:04) follows. It ends on a long-deferred major-key cadence, which the band approaches via the work's recurring, chordal turning point. The band emphasizes the unusual ending of the end of section 5 through a sustained hard rock flourish, including a gong-like sound.

Section 6, "The Sphere—A Kind of Dream" (17:04–18:08), inscribes yet another major-key tonality. However, the band places an unexpected chord in the middle of the section, just after lyrics about pursuing a "different aim." The meaning is that Cygnus has balanced and enriched both Apollo/Mind/Wisdom and Dionysus/Heart/Love. The section also features a clean-timbred guitar sound, Lee's normal/lower countertenor, and a warm keyboard countermelody. It has no distorted electric guitar, no bass guitar, and no drums. It provides a safe, normative folk-rock sound. The lyrics call for "truth [and] sensibility, armed with sense and liberty, with the Heart and Mind united in a single perfect sphere." Ideally, we would all manage to bridge these two things.

The Rest of *Hemispheres*

In a more modest idiom, the second half of *Hemispheres* opens with "Circumstances" (3:44). It is a hard rock anthem (something like *2112*'s "Something for Nothing") and deals with youthful naïveté transforming into adult idealism. The words include some French: "Plus ça change, plus c'est la meme chose," which means: "The more things change, the more they stay the same." Around this time, the band members studied French, and Neil Peart bought a mountain-area lake house in Quebec as a second home. (Peart's family mainly lived in Toronto's Forest Hill, Lee's lived in Toronto's Rosedale, and Lifeson's lived mainly north of Toronto.) In addition, Rush then recorded its 1980–1984 and 1989–1993 studio albums at a major studio (Le Studio) not far from Peart's house in Quebec. "Circumstances" was a bit unusual, though.

Rush's music more often had to do with individualism, forging a professional and/or personal identity, and not allowing outside forces to control one's activities and path. The rest of the album definitely did so,
though.

"The Trees"

The third song on *Hemispheres*, "The Trees" (4:45) inscribes a pointed
criticism of legislated equality (artificial "balance"). Its lyrics present an
allegory depicting one group of trees, the Maples, as being oppressed
by another group of trees, the more lofty Oaks. The maple leaf functions as Canada's most important national symbol. Thus, one might
reasonably interpret the Maples in this song as Canada and the Oaks as
the United States. This makes sense at an initial level of inquiry, and
Rush does not privilege the Oaks.

In 1971, Canada introduced cultural content regulations in the form
of broadcasting quotas set at 30 percent Canadian content ("CanCon").
A "Canadian" recording features at least two of the following four categories being provided by Canadians: music, artist, production, and lyrics. (In a cheesy pun, it almost spells "maple.") However, Rush's aggressive touring and stylistically varied album catalog enabled its continuing
success in the United States, the UK, elsewhere, *and* Canada—despite
any such regulations. In "The Trees," the Maples form a union and an
outside force ultimately cuts the Oaks down to the height of the Maples. The closing lyrics of the song—"and the trees are all kept equal by
hatchet, axe, and saw"—make it quite clear that Rush considers the
solution inappropriate. Whether or not Rush meant anything particularly Canadian by it, the song includes numerous ironic inscriptions of
artificial balance, and the sentiment is very libertarian.

"The Trees" demonstrates the compact approach that Rush used
while also continuing with certain extended works between 1975 and
1981. With a duration of less than five minutes, the song succinctly
distributes vocal and instrumental passages, nearly balances unison and
contrapuntal instrumental sections, uses a wide variety of time signatures, includes quite a lot of synthesizer material, and varies considerably in dynamics. It begins with Lifeson's classical-guitar introduction
(0:00–0:10). He had recently taken some classical-guitar lessons. After
the introduction (which is in 6/8 time), the same music underlies the

first verse (0:10–0:22), with Lee joining on bass and vocals. He provides a fairly straightforward bass part and sings in his natural baritone register. The music moves between related keys (mostly in minor), but with some insinuations of additional tonal areas. Lee sings about the "unrest" of the Maples' discontent, and he adjusts certain rhythms in order to highlight the idea within the continuing 6/8 time.

Bird sounds (similar to water/nature sounds in Rush's earlier "2112" and "Xanadu") play up the idea of a "state of nature" in which the Oaks ignore the Maples' pleas. As Lee sings "Oaks ignore their pleas" in the last phrase, he shifts his rhythmic emphasis into a kind of "taunting" gesture (similar to "nya-nya-nya-nya-nya"). The band had earlier used similar gestures in "Working Man" and "Anthem." In any case, verse 1 enacts a precarious balance. Lifeson and Lee then reinforce the idea by repeating the verse music ("A") instrumentally, but with Lee compensating for his lack of vocals by playing a more active bass-guitar part (0:22–0:34). A brief segment (0:34–0:40) then summarizes the "balancing act" but subtly shifts the time signature into 3/4 instead of 6/8.

Less subtly, the following section ("B") suddenly changes a number of things (starting at 0:40–0:47). Lifeson shifts to heavy, strummed, rhythmically regular power chords in a more major-key area, and Peart begins some powerful drumming. The quarter-note pulse of 3/4 time is immediately shifted into 4/4, and additional chords are also introduced. Lee sings verse 2 (about the Oaks being too lofty, 0:47–1:15) in his piercing countertenor voice—much higher than he has just been singing. The beginning of the song is quite pastoral, but this section uses an agitated, urgent, heavy metal style. Also, certain chords and tonal areas depict the song's ongoing differentiation between the neighboring Maples and Oaks.

A brief interlude appears (1:15–1:21); then this time the second A section (verse 3, 1:21–1:45, and back in 6/8 time) noticeably retains the heavy metal style of the song's B section. By now, the "creatures all have fled," perhaps frightened away by the Maples' screams of "oppression." This time, too, the shift to 4/4 after the verse establishes not the B section, but an extended instrumental section. It begins with a melancholy, woodwind-like, synthesizer solo (1:45–2:17) that moves from its tonal area to a chord that strongly reinforces it. Meanwhile, Lifeson plays reflective electric-guitar figurations. Peart plays rhythmic, woodblock drum sounds that evoke hammering woodpeckers. A passage in a time signature with an added beat (5/4, 2:17–2:53) shifts the harmony back to where it was. The music then becomes louder and quite rhythmic (2:53–3:10). Lee plays bass patterns something like what he *sang* in verse 1 (the A section). The overall effect of the section is one of a compromise between the A and B sections, and it also includes Lifeson's guitar solo (3:10–3:29) over the continuing 5/4 material.

After the solo, a segment in 6/8 (3:29–3:49) then further recalls the formerly sung rhythms. However, in it the band expands the song's "balance" motif with brief, "stop-time" ascending versus descending passages in the bass and guitar—alongside Peart's continuing woodblocks. It effect is one of a heated, contrapuntal volley of conflicting arguments. The section then returns to the earlier 5/4 riff (3:49–3:58) from which it emerged.

The second B section of "The Trees" (verse 4, 3:58–4:28) follows, with the Maples forming a union and "demanding equal rights." At the end of the verse (4:20–4:23), Lee noticeably sings equal quarter-note rhythms on the words "trees are all kept equal" on a single pitch. His vocal gesture on those words means that the external agents then mentioned ("hatchet, axe, and saw," by way of a "noble law") have artificially brought about "equality." There is no return to 6/8 time, and the song ends abruptly on an unexpected chord. In addition, the song's coda (4:28–4:42) reprises the "state of nature" bird sounds from the song's opening, and it also includes Peart's weirdly ominous wind chime effects. These ending gestures mean that the song's ultimate solution is not any more natural than the situation at the beginning of the song and that there has to be a better way than trying to make everyone the same. Although the song does mention a union, it is not "anti-union" so much as it is a presentation of a more general libertarian view about the artificiality of external powers, legislated equality, and so on.

"La Villa Strangiato"

Rush intersperses the main vocal sections of their songs with extensive instrumental sections. These include introductions, transitions, virtuosic interplays, middle sections, and solos. So, it was probably inevitable that the band would eventually compose some entirely instrumental narratives. "La Villa Strangiato" (9:34), the closing "epic instrumental" of *Hemispheres*, comes complete with elaborate section headings as well as the caveat "An Exercise in Self-Indulgence." (See textbox below for an overview of the various sections of "La Villa Strangiato.")

Overview of "La Villa Strangiato" (from *Hemispheres*, 1978)
The sections are based on the lyrics–sheet liner notes.

La Villa Strangiato
(An Exercise in Self–Indulgence)
Including

Buenos Nochas, Mein Froinds! (0:00–0:26)
To sleep, perchance to dream . . . (0:26–2:00)
Strangiato Theme (2:00–3:16)
A Lerxst in Wonderland (3:16–5:49)
Monsters! (5:49–6:10)
The Ghost of the Aragon (6:10–6:46)
Danforth and Pape (6:46–7:27)
The Waltz of the Shreves (7:27–7:53)
Never Turn Your Back on a Monster! (7:53–8:04)
Monsters! (Reprise) (8:04–8:18)
Strangiato Theme (Reprise) (8:18–9:22)
A Farewell to Things (9:22–9:34)

The title "La Villa Strangiato" intentionally conflates not-quite French with not-quite Spanish (or possibly not-quite Italian), and it is supposed to mean "The Strange City." In this case, "villa" is pronounced "via," like "ville" (French for "city"), rather than "villa" (i.e., an estate). "Strangiato" is not actually a word in any language.

Like the work's main title, the title of section 1 ("Buenos Nochas, Mein Froinds!") combines two languages, this time poor Spanish with something like German or Yiddish. (Lee and Lifeson both had parents who immigrated to Canada from eastern Europe.) Lifeson bases his simple, opening classical-guitar gesture on the melody of "Gute Nacht, Freunde," by A. Yondrascheck. Broken chords, slightly elaborated the third time, resolve on strummed ones (0:00–0:21). This tactic may relate to the Yiddish/German part of the section's title. Lifeson explained that the sections of the work emerged from some of his strange dreams. Section 1's title and Yondrascheck's gentle tune both evoke a lullaby or "night prayers." Thus, the work's opening may relate to a childhood dream, or later childlike dream, experienced by Lifeson. He follows this with an extremely fast, flamenco-like passage, descending from a relatively high pitch down almost two octaves to the root of a major chord (0:21–0:26). This evokes the Spanish part of section 1's title, but it also suggests falling into sleep or, perhaps, into a more intense dream.

Section 2 ("To sleep, perchance to dream . . . ," 0:26–2:00, in 4/4 time) is named after a line from Hamlet's "To be or not to be" soliloquy in Shakespeare's play. It grows from a lullaby-like "extended major" chord. This includes a repeated, descending ostinato "lulling" in its upper register. The section slowly becomes louder and more active, including bell, synthesizer, and, eventually, bass-guitar gestures and ever more intricate drum patterns. This part of the dream remains incomplete and ambiguous. Suddenly, the "Strangiato Theme" (section 3, 2:00–3:16, also in 4/4 time) interrupts the ambiguous dream. This music features much more clearly delineated sections, involving gentle syncopations alternating with frenetic descents. The second half of the work's main theme includes a brief angular passage (2:25–2:38 and 2:57–3:10) that oscillates harshly across a tritone. The band follows the second such passage with a coda (3:10–3:16) that comprises a four-measure restatement of the earlier, frenetic, descending guitar gesture. However, section 4 suddenly aborts this.

Section 4, "A Lerxst in Wonderland" (3:16–5:49) references Lifeson's "band nickname." It slows down the rhythmic activity but switches the time signature to 7/4. It also alternates the pitch level between a major chord and its "flat six." This relationship traditionally encodes "illusory hope" (as it does in earlier Rush songs), and thus it may here suggest the impossibility of escaping from "Wonderland." Lifeson (Lerxst) plays an emotive, bluesy guitar solo (3:39–5:14) over these continuing changes. In it, he features slow-delay note-attacks in which he uses the guitar's volume control to introduce pitches hesitantly and "unnaturally." The continuing "flat six" motions and the note delays combine to give this section a disembodied, dreamlike quality. It falls somewhere between the earlier dream section and the clearer elements of the main theme (section 3). After the hesitancy and occasionally abrupt flourishes of the solo, the section builds in texture and volume in its final measures (5:14–5:49), thereby recalling section 2's building dream effects). The dream thus begins to approach its most intense phase.

Rush based the melody of "Monsters!" (section 5, 5:49–6:10) on the main tune of the second section of "Powerhouse" (1937) by the U.S. bandleader Raymond Scott (1908–1994). This appropriation eventually got Rush in some legal trouble, but the parties resolved it out of court. The tune would have been familiar to Rush through its frequent use as "mechanical music" in 1950s Warner Bros. cartoons. For example, one such cartoon uses this music (with its characteristic tritone) for a conveyor-belt assembly line of hens laying eggs. Rush initially alters Scott's tune to conform to the band's characteristic 7/8. However, the band then reverts to the original's 4/4 and combines it with guitar trills on the ending note, a related bass line, a frenetic cadential gesture, and alternate ending pitches. The combination of these things provides an unsettling effect, similar to the most intense phase of REM (rapid eye movement) sleep. The physical effects of REM sleep thus inspired the comparative clarity of this section of "La Villa Strangiato." In this section, Lifeson and Lee also use the technique of "palm-muting" and force the melody's opening three notes *not* to resonate. This approach parallels the staccato delivery of these same notes in Scott's equally eccentric original. The frenetic effects contribute to the short-lived, intense images of REM sleep.

Section 6, "The Ghost of the Aragon" (6:10–6:46, back to 4/4 time), retains the feverish aesthetic of "Monsters!" It begins with a brief, virtuosic bass solo that rises, partly via tritones, in its first measure. It then descends in its second measure. The section continues with vivid, clear, and highly syncopated open chords that chromatically descend by an octave over two measures. Then, the texture becomes increasingly spotty and "guttural." The section ends suddenly on a cadence that implies an impending return to the key of the main Strangiato theme. However, the band first works through some additional material and reprises. The Aragon Ballroom is a large, well-known music venue in Chicago, which originally opened in 1926 as an extravagant jazz-era theater. Rush played there eight times between 1974 and early 1978.

A brief drum solo leads into section 7 ("Danforth and Pape," 6:46–7:27). Here, the band plays quite chromatically. In particular, Lifeson provides a hard rock guitar solo over highly syncopated, dissonant changes that also incorporate extended chords. Danforth and Pape is an intersection in a historically Greek neighborhood northeast of downtown Toronto. Section 8 ("The Waltz of the Shreves," 7:27–7:53) features triple-beat—hence "waltz" (a triple-beat dance)—largely unison passages. Section 9 ("Never Turn Your Back on a Monster!" 7:53–8:04) comprises a brief, bluesy, 6/8 version of the bass pattern from the earlier "Monsters!" section. Section 10 ("Monsters! [Reprise]," 8:04–8:18) reprises the 4/4 part of "Monsters!" As its title suggests, the "Strangiato Theme (Reprise)" (section 11, 8:18–9:22), returns to the work's main theme. At the beginning of section 12 ("A Farewell to Things," 9:22–9:34), the band reprises the 7/8 part of the "Monsters!" section, as well as the chromatic descent from section 6 and a final, single-measure, ascending-then-descending bass solo that recalls the beginning of section 6. "A Farewell to Things" references Rush's 1977 album and album title song, "A Farewell to Kings." The "cheeky," self-effacing quip probably suggests that the band had a good sense that it would begin to move in a post-progressive direction on its next album. Indeed, the work ends abruptly on a staccato chord, as though suddenly awakening from a dream.

"La Villa Strangiato" achieves its indulgent, musicianly effects though an ebbing and flowing among comparatively clear versus ambiguous elements. However, the sectionalized, modular nature of the work suggests that Rush wished to construct it as a comparatively left-brain (rational, logical) activity. The work thus arguably relates more to Apollonian (mind/wisdom) than Dionysian (heart/love) tendencies. On the whole, though, the band continued its struggle to bring those elements into balance, even in its subsequent instrumental works. Also, around the same time as *Hemispheres*, Rush's first three albums (1974–1975) were rereleased as a boxed LP set, *Archives* (1978). That was done to capitalize on the band's first breakthrough that had started with *2112* (1976).

PERMANENT WAVES (1980)

Rush's second breakthrough came in the early 1980s, beginning with *Permanent Waves* (1980). The album includes the succinctly individualist songs "The Spirit of Radio" and "Freewill," but also the mini-epic "Natural Science." The band recorded the album in the summer of

1979 at Le Studio near Morin Heights, Quebec, coproducing it with long-term colleague Terry Brown and recording it with engineer Paul Northfield. The release of *Permanent Waves* was timed so that it would be the very first major label album released in the new decade, and the album appeared in stores on New Year's Day, 1980.

The album cover, by Hugh Syme (with input by Neil Peart), shows a hurricane that has destroyed buildings, flooded streets, and so on. The original photograph was taken by Flip Schulke at the Galveston, Texas, Seawall during 1961's Hurricane Carla. In the foreground, Syme places a beautiful young woman (portrayed by model Paula Turnbull) smiling toward the camera and walking past us. Her wavy, "perm" (permanent wave) hairdo provides a visual pun on the album title, and her Marilyn Monroe–like, blown-up dress—revealing her legs and panties—suggest a classic, continuing idea of value and beauty. Her progress, through the frame, means that worthy ideals can survive an apparently devastating storm and make it through even particularly heavy flood waves.

In the distant left of the album cover, a man—possibly a crossing guard (portrayed by cover artist Hugh Syme)—waves (in another pun) off into the distance and perhaps seems to have encouraged a fearless response to the storm, with his other hand on a "Walk—Cross Here" sign. In the distant right, still-standing business signs subtly show the names "Lee," "Peart," and "Lifeson." One of the signs in the original photograph was for Coca-Cola, but the company refused to allow it to be shown. The album title is also barely visible, as it is incorporated along a visual representation of a waveform. The band name is much clearer. Most of the album cover is in black and white, but the band name and album title include some color. The "model" beauty (literally), the fearless/waving man, the band members' tiny/self-effacing names, and the prominence of "Rush" over the album title all give the sense that the band's new music is still going to make sense as Rush.

The album cover's storm represents the dramatic changes of post-punk and other post-progressive music in the late 1970s and early 1980s, including their stripped-down textures and concise song structures. However, the image's other, more subtle elements suggest that Rush intends to remain standing in such a context. The band knew that sympathetic critics and fans might react negatively to its new, "post-prog" approach. Likewise, it knew that its detractors might actually find the band's new music more acceptable, but without fully understanding the things that gave it continuity with Rush's earlier music. In other words, either group might "get it wrong." So, the album cover also incorporates one of the most famous examples of getting it wrong. It references the *Chicago Tribune* having declared the incorrect winner in the 1948 U.S. presidential election: "Dewey Defeats Truman." The newspaper forced the headline to be blocked out in the United States, but hundreds of thousands of non-U.S. LPs retained it in modified form: "Dewei Defeats Truman."

"The Spirit of Radio"

The album's opening song, "The Spirit of Radio" (4:59) functioned as a rallying cry for the band to continue releasing new music into the 1980s. The band wondered whether or not it would be able to update its sound while simultaneously retaining its mark of complex rhythms and instrumental virtuosity. "The Spirit of Radio," though, brought Rush's streamlined progressive power trio aesthetic (including virtuosic unisons, short/vivid guitar solos, succinct use of "odd meters," and subtle synthesizers) into the larger mainstream while also bringing the larger mainstream (e.g., "modern rock," such as by the Police) into Rush.

In the late 1970s and early 1980s, the phrase "The Spirit of Radio" signified the Toronto-area "modern/new" free-form radio station 102.1 CFNY (later called "The Edge" and "Edge 102"), and the station played post-punk, blues, jazz, reggae, other world music, and so on—to which the members of Rush listened. The station modeled itself after New York City "indie rock" (the mecca being the underground rock club CBGB, 1973–), and the "NY" part of the station name specifically referenced "New York." These are the types of music the members of Rush were listening to around 1979–1980, even if most of its fans were not.

Late-1970s punk rock prided itself on its stripped-down aesthetic and its anarchic, intentionally "unprofessional" demeanor. This represented the antithesis of progressive rock. However, within a few years, certain post-punk, pop-punk, and new-wave musicians demonstrated that they were *also* capable of constructing and playing structurally and rhythmically complicated music. For example, Talking Heads collaborated from 1978 to 1981 with "art rock"/minimalist/ambient musician-producer Brian Eno. The Police's guitarist Andy Summers collaborated with Robert Fripp, guitarist-founder of the seminal progressive rock band King Crimson. Fripp and Eno also worked together in the 1970s. This music differs from Rush's late-1970s progressive hard fusion largely because it centers on minimalist-influenced interlocking rhythmic patterns. However, it represented one of the more fruitful directions for post-progressive artists of the 1980s, including Peter Gabriel and Rush.

"The Spirit of Radio" provides a very good example of a sound with guitar and drums interacting, and many of its recurring gestures display a raw, backbeat energy that fits perfectly with the aesthetic of early-1980s, post-punk music—which was itself influenced by reggae. However, Rush consistently combines this energy with its unique hybrid of progressive rock and hard rock and with its ongoing penchant for virtuosity. With the single exception of a brief 7/4 instrumental break near the middle of the song, "The Spirit of Radio" remains entirely in 4/4. Until the mid-1980s, this would prove unusual among Rush's most highly regarded songs. In the instrumental sections before and between vocal sections, the virtuosic elements continue the somewhat modular approach of "La Villa Strangiato" (instrumental, 1978). They also anticipate the energy-meets-virtuosity aesthetic of "YYZ" (instrumental, 1981). Such elements include unison versus contrapuntal aspects, syncopations, rhythm (but not meter) changes, and changes in instrumentation.

Seventies hard rock often used "modes," whereas post-punk and early-1980s new wave often used major and minor keys. Not surprisingly, Rush combines these in "The Spirit of Radio." The song's circular energy riff (0:00–0:17) and repeated, syncopated, semichromatic, unison ascent (0:17–0:27) are modal and/or 1970s sounding. By comparison, the song's verses are clearly in a major key. The lyrics of the first two verses (0:27–1:24) recount one's favorite disc jockey being an "unobtrusive companion" who plays "magic music [to] make your morning mood." After an instrumental break on the same chord progression, verse 2 resumes as the narrator encourages you to go "off on your way" in the "happy solitude" of your car. The rhythmic anticipations provide a lilting joy, as though driving while listening to the radio is a ritual to be savored.

After verse 2, Lifeson reprises the song's circular, opening, modal energy riff. Lee adds a simple, staccato accompanying gesture and a slow-moving, string-like ascent-descent on synthesizers. He reports that he originated these synthesizer parts as keyboard sequences (i.e., digitally recorded them) and then "wrote the bass and guitar lines to fit the sequences" (Armbruster 1984, 60). The sequences build in intensity to accompany the song's chorus, where Lee sings Peart's lyrics about "invisible airwaves," "antennas," "bristling energy," and "emotional feedback" (1:24–1:52). Verse 3 is in a hard rock style, and it explains the stylistic compromise: "All this machinery making modern music can still be openhearted." However, the lyrics also note that "glittering prizes and endless compromises shatter the illusion of integrity" (1:52–2:27). The synth-heavy chorus is then repeated (2:27–2:53).

The song's middle section (2:53–3:18) then reminds the listener that it really is still by Rush. The band shifts into 7/4 time and into 1970s-style harmonic complexities and modes. After an instrumental hard rock version of the verse (3:18–3:32), Lifeson returns to the song's circular, modal energy riff. However, the band quickly aborts it for a return (3:32–3:49) to materials from the beginning of the song—the virtuosic unison and semichromatic, unison ascent. None of this music sounds much like the early 1980s, and Rush could have ended the song after it. However, the band wanted to solidify its point about not compromising its integrity despite doing new things.

Toward the end of the song (3:49–4:18), the band inserts two statements of its diatonic, major-key verse material—but in a kind of reggae style. Rush's earlier music did not indicate the possibility of a stylistic move in this direction. Peart's words in this part of the song actually derive from part of the lyrics of Simon and Garfunkel's 1965 song "The Sounds of Silence." He accuses the music industry of focusing too narrowly on "the words of the profits," by which he means that music industry executives fail to live up to Paul Simon's subway/tenement "prophets." (Ironically, Simon and Garfunkel's original folk song had itself been modified by producers, etc., to include rock instruments—bass and drums.)

In the "reggae" sections of "The Spirit of Radio" Geddy Lee usually sings in his natural chest voice, which sounds like he's being quite laid back. Similarly, the band plays in a more "stripped-down" (less "busy") manner, even with stylized backbeats and reggae-inspired, post-punk steel-drum sounds. The second pseudo-reggae section attacks the unpleasant music industry, and Lee spits out the word "salesmen." Alex Lifeson's angry, bluesy, wah-wah-effected guitar solo (4:18–4:36) then angrily caricatures the chattering arguments of such people. For the song's second reprise of its main, unison, hard rock ascent, the band's cover artist Hugh Syme plays a comparatively simple "rock-and-roll piano" part in order to further heighten the stylistic ambiguity. Rush normally used keyboards for occasional melodic, timbral, or textural reasons, not for this sort of rhythmic rock and roll. The song ends (4:36–4:56) with a piano-accompanied version of the ascent, a final reprise of the energy riff, and an energetic ending cadence.

Rush immediately strove to explore certain things about "The Spirit of Radio" in nearly all of their subsequent music. For example, from 1981 to 2012 the band's new songs averaged only around five minutes in duration. In addition, Rush continued to make space for their virtuosity, to use different types of complex rhythms, to build songs through recurring ("modular") gestures and sections, to address relatively serious topics, to incorporate music technology, and to acknowledge other types of music. Rush continued to do these things for several decades and thus continued to denote "progressive rock." It did so long after most of the earlier British progressive rock bands (e.g., Yes and Genesis) no longer made that kind of music.

Rush's fellow Toronto compatriots the Barenaked Ladies featured a version of the energy riff from "The Spirit of Radio" (along with material derived from Rush's 1981 song "Tom Sawyer") in their song "Grade 9" (pop-rock, *Gordon*, 1992). Their song references the socially awkward early years of high school for "geeky" aspiring rock musicians— such as themselves. Classical musicians also responded to the song, including Rachel Barton's instrumental cover version (live string trio, *Stringendo: Storming the Citadel*, 1997–1998), a less-effective one in the "String Tribute" series (*Exit . . . Stage Right: The String Quartet Tribute to Rush*, 2002), and another by the Royal Philharmonic Orchestra (. . . *Plays the Music of Rush*, 2012). In another vein, the heavy metal band Premonition made a more conventional cover version (on the multiartist album *Red Star: Tribute to Rush*, 1999), and Jeff Stinco and Kip Winger made a vaguely similar version (on the multiartist album, *Subdivisions: A Tribute to the Music of Rush*, 2005).

The Rest of *Permanent Waves*

"Freewill" (5:24) is the second song on *Permanent Waves*. It criticizes those who allow themselves to be manipulated as "playthings" of unearthly powers or fate instead of taking responsibility for their own actions. The tagline of the individualist chorus exemplifies this: "I will choose a path that's clear; I will choose free will." The song's musical gestures provide a high degree of "progressive" elements—virtuosity, elaborate counterpoint among the instruments, shifting time signatures, and four tonal areas.

The first half of *Permanent Waves* ends with the nature/storm-themed, mainly instrumental, and metrically complex "Jacob's Ladder" (7:28). The opening pair of songs on the second half of *Permanent Waves* comprise "Entre Nous" (4:37, only the title is in French) and "Different Strings" (3:50, lyrics by Lee). Both provide positive viewpoints on "differences within relationships" and use 4/4 time. The latter includes contributions on grand piano by Hugh Syme, and the band thus intended it as a studio-only production number. *Permanent Waves* (1980), like *A Farewell to Kings* (1977) and *Hemispheres* (1978), concludes with a moderate-length extended work.

"Natural Science" (9:17), Rush's penultimate extended work, reflects one of the band's most diverse statements, both lyrically and instrumentally. The work includes nature sounds and folklike acoustic guitar sections as well as some of the band's most rhythmically complex and timbrally heavy playing. Lyrically and musically, the work reflects an anxiety over science and technology, as in: "Science like nature must also be tamed." It begins with the sounds of water and birds, and tide pools represent the basic building blocks of humanity throughout the work. However, 7/8 time and electronically derived sounds in the two middle verses ("Hyperspace") represent a "mechanized world out of hand." Overall, the work espouses the honesty of the individual ("Art as expression, not as market campaigns"), and thus it relates to verse 3 of the same album's opening song, "The Spirit of Radio" (e.g., "All this machinery making modern music can still be openhearted"). Rush has a reputation for long songs. However, "Natural Science" and the lesser-known "The Camera Eye" (1981, 11:01) are the band's last two new studio songs over 7:31 in duration. That is true even though the band wrote and recorded 115 new songs in the thirty years from 1982 to 2012.

CODA

By 1978–1979, Rush toured exclusively as a headlining act, though sometimes in "second-tier" venues and smaller cities. By then, it had a substantial, professional road crew for instrument setup and maintenance, sound, lighting, and so on. Reflecting the band's transition from rather extreme forms of progressive rock and individualism in the late 1970s to more modest, post-progressive songs in the early 1980s, the stylistic context for the band's music became increasingly diverse. For example, from 1978 to 1980 Rush's opening acts still included AC/DC, Cheap Trick, and Max Webster. However, they also included UFO (British, hard rock and heavy metal), Golden Earring (Dutch, progressive-influenced pop-rock), and the Pat Travers Band (Canadian, blues-oriented rock).

4

"MODERN-DAY WARRIOR"

User-Friendly Progressive Rock
and *Moving Pictures*, 1981

Rush's second breakthrough happened in the period from 1980 to 1985. The band began to make more of its songs structurally modest, but it still included various technical complexities and lyrically continued to deal with relatively serious matters. The band had released quite a few lengthy songs between 1974 and 1980. Its fifteen longest songs in that period average 10:43, with two of the longest ones, "2112" (20:33) and "Hemispheres" (18:08), opening the albums named after them. However, in the same period the group also had twenty-eight songs averaging only 3:56. In 1980–1981, though, Rush became more consistently accessible, opening its albums with distinctive, relatively short songs and not writing any more long songs after 1981. The band's most commercially successful album of its career is *Moving Pictures* (1981).

MOVING PICTURES (1981)

After its progressive rock of the 1970s, Rush took its music into a "post-progressive" direction. However, its work as a whole (1974–2012) has since been reclaimed as progressive rock, and the "perfect storm" of *Moving Pictures* (1981, recorded at Quebec's Le Studio and co-produced by Terry Brown) is at the heart of that attitude. For most people, even more than thirty years later, it is probably the best place to start listening to Rush. The band may have thought so itself, as it played the entire album live for the very first time on its 2010–2011 tours, as a thirtieth birthday present for itself and its fans. In 1995, the Recording Industry Association of America (RIAA) certified *Moving Pictures* as quadruple platinum: four million copies sold in the United States. The RIAA had earlier certified the album gold and platinum in 1981 and double platinum in 1984. The album gained its favorable reputation largely based on the four songs on its first half: "Tom Sawyer," "Red Barchetta," the instrumental "YYZ," and "Limelight." These continue the succinct individualism embodied in 1980's "The Spirit of Radio" and "Freewill," but they also pursue a more picturesque (or personal) idiom in keeping with the album title's filmic reference.

Hugh Syme's album cover for *Moving Pictures* combines a title pun on the band's early 1980s cinematic/picturesque approach to songwriting with a multiple visual play on words: people moved emotionally by pictures being moved physically. The front picture depicts Joan of Arc (portrayed by one of Syme's associates), the middle picture reproduces C. M. Coolidge's *A Friend in Need* (a.k.a. *Dogs Playing Poker*), and the rear picture comprises the man-against-star logo of Rush's album *2112* (1976). These appear in front of the distinctive three-arch entrance of the Ontario Provincial Legislature in Toronto's Queen's Park. The three pictures and the three arches also visually play on the fact that Rush comprises three members, a recurring motif on Rush's album covers in the 1980s and 1990s.

"Tom Sawyer"

Moving Pictures opens with "Tom Sawyer" (4:33, lyrics cowritten by Pye Dubois), which is Rush's best-known song. It begins in a fairly straightforward manner, with the band at first acting somewhat reserved, in the same way that Mark Twain's original character sometimes has to interact politely with others. Geddy Lee's synthesizer filter sweep and Neil Peart's sparse drumming in 2/2, "cut," or "marchlike" time function like a fanfare, immediately marking the song as "different" from any of Rush's earlier music. Lee's vocal introduction describes the song's modern-day Tom Sawyer as a warrior, with a "mean, mean stride" and a "mean, mean pride."

The underlying music then changes to follow the idea of stride-meets-pride, mostly through Alex Lifeson's guitar-chord progression that sounds, appropriately, like a confident "swagger." Verse 1 suggests our hero's "mind is not for rent," but also clarifies that he doesn't really mean to be arrogant. By analogy to the original's raft, the new Tom Sawyer rides out his life on "the river" of complex, modern society. Extending the river/raft analogy, the song's prechorus and chorus are more dreamlike, with words about mystery; the world, love, and life are "deep," and the skies are "wide." The song also suggests that we are all a part of this depth and wideness, and a new version of the song's vocal introduction suggests that Tom Sawyer gets his energy from "you"—as in, anyone listening.

An extended instrumental section further explores the ideas of confidence, depth, and looking outside of ourselves. It features one of the band's uses of an unusual time signature: 7/4, instead of the rest of the song's much more normal-sounding 2/2. The section begins with Lee's descending melodic pattern on a synthesizer. However, it soon becomes "traditional Rush," when he takes over his own pattern on bass guitar, in order to support Lifeson's guitar solo. The solo is quite complex, with unexpected leaps and rhythms and with string bends alternating with fast patterns. The solo ends when Lifeson joins in with Lee's underlying pattern; and Peart also matches them rhythmically in his drumming. As with Twain's Tom Sawyer, sometimes we have to do our own thing in eccentric counterpoint to what others are doing, and sometimes we have to come together and do much the same thing as everyone else.

To get back to the song's earlier music (and "cut" time), the band restates the "swagger" progression. However, this time it features Peart's drumming prowess quite prominently, in a kind of "mini drum solo." Verse 2 refers to the quite libertarian notion of neither god nor government being worthy of our modern Tom Sawyer's mind and also to the idea of him being "hopeful, yet discontent" and having change as a permanent, overall strategy. The instrumental verse, prechorus, and chorus all then each happen one more time, but note that the words of the prechorus and chorus are changed slightly.

An expanded, ending version of the vocal "introduction" then prepares the song's exit, so that we can all get on with "the friction of the day." Tellingly, the song ends with a version of its 7/4 instrumental section. The ending grooves along, but it also fades out—as though we're all drifting away on modern-day river rafts while also still managing to cause some mischief of our own. (Indeed, the album's very next song is a near-future one about the pleasures of illegally racing around the countryside in a powerful and well-preserved sports car.) Of course, we're meant to understand that the band itself is one of many possible modern-day Tom Sawyers. But so are you!

Sightings of "Tom Sawyer," 1992–2012

"Tom Sawyer" appeared in three major motion pictures in 1998 alone: *Small Soldiers*, *The Waterboy*, and *Whatever*. Joe Dante's *Small Soldiers* combines human characters and computer-animated toy characters. High-tech gadgetry, including "real" intelligence, animates the title characters and their toy enemies. The main teenage boy and girl characters are social misfits, somewhat rebellious, and attempt to solve the mystery of the toys' "magical" power, which, needless to say, gets out of hand. The filmmakers of *Small Soldiers* suggest the possibility that rebellious, suburban ("Tom Sawyer") teenagers in 1998 might very well listen to hard rock music from 1969 to 1987. However, the rock music selections in this film, as well as Jerry Goldsmith's self-referential uses of his score for *Patton* (WWII film, 1970), and of Wagner's "Ride of the Valkyries" (referencing similar helicopter scenes in *Apocalypse Now*, 1979), suggest that the filmmakers had a multigenerational audience in mind. In order to appeal to the film's younger audience, the CD "soundtrack" consists of a series of ten late-1990s hip-hop remixes of most of the classic rock songs used in the film. DJ Z-Trip's remix of "Tom Sawyer" gives the original's 7/4 instrumental gesture two extra eighth notes and also simplifies most of the song's drum parts, thus largely erasing any vestiges of progressive rock. By comparison, his updated guitar bridge, scratching effects, vocal manipulations, and chord resequencings succeed better in reanimating the original. Ironically, the remix extends the song by two minutes (6:33 vs. 4:33), which counters Rush's own considerable efforts toward relatively concise forms during the era of its original version of the song.

The 1998 Adam Sandler comedy *The Waterboy*, directed by Frank Coraci, uses Rush's "Tom Sawyer" to underscore a montage establishing Sandler's misfit title character as a football tackling star. The character becomes an unlikely hero when angered, and like the "modern-day warrior" of Rush's song he has a "mean, mean stride" and a "mean, mean pride." Like the earlier Tom Sawyers (Mark Twain's and Rush's), Sandler's character revels in friction instead of trading away his energy. Susan Skoog sets her independent film *Whatever* (1998) in suburban New Jersey in the year of Rush's actual song—1981. "Tom Sawyer" functions as the featured song in establishing the mood and setting for the first of the film's numerous party scenes, where half-drunk/half-stoned teenage potheads debate the relative merits of free will and Ronald Reagan. The entire soundtrack resonates with punk, mainstream post-punk ("new wave"), "early alternative," art rock/pop, and mainstream heavy metal songs heard in numerous suburban contexts in the early 1980s. "Tom Sawyer" also appears in *Halloween* (the updated version by Rob Zombie, 2007), *Fanboys* (2009), *I Love You, Man* (also 2009), and in episodes of the TV shows *Chuck*, *Family Guy*, *Freaks and Geeks*, and *Futurama*. In addition, the band played the song live on *The Colbert Report* in 2008, not to mention in every one of the well over one thousand major-venue concerts that it performed from 1981 to 2013. In addition, the Rush-fan creators of the TV show *South Park* created the short film *Lil' Rush* (featuring the show's characters playing a version of Rush's "Tom Sawyer") that was used during the band's 2007–2008 tour in support of *Snakes & Arrows* (2007).

As for cover versions of "Tom Sawyer," a death metal version by Disarray (on the multiartist album *Red Star: Tribute to Rush*, 1999) features grunted or "demonic" vocals. It not only transforms the 7/4 section into 4/4 (as with the *Small Soldiers* remix), but it *also* slows it down. Other cover versions of "Tom Sawyer" include the ones by Death Organ (progressive heavy metal, *Universal Stripsearch*, 1997); Deadsy (alternative/industrial, *Commencement*, 2002); the "String Tribute" series (classical strings, *Exit . . . Stage Right: The String Quartet Tribute to Rush*, 2002); Sebastian Bach, Dominic Cifarelli, and Jeff Feldman (on the multiartist album *Subdivisions: A Tribute to the Music of Rush*, 2005); Mindless Self Indulgence (industrial metal, *You'll Rebel to Anything*, 2006); the Bad Plus (jazz-pop, *Prog*, 2007); and the Royal Philharmonic Orchestra (classical, *. . . Plays the Music of Rush*, 2012). Many Rush songs appear in cover versions on similar tribute albums (including *Working Man: A Tribute to Rush*, various artists, 1996), on the interactive video game *Rock Band 2*, and played by dozens of live, Rush

tribute bands. However, "The Spirit of Radio" (1980) and "Tom Sawyer" (1981) are the most commonly covered Rush songs, at least on
officially released recordings.

The song has also been referenced by other artists and in other
contexts. As mentioned earlier, Toronto's Barenaked Ladies use the
swagger progression of "Tom Sawyer" (along with the "energy riff" of
"The Spirit of Radio") in their song "Grade 9" (pop-rock, *Gordon*,
1992). Metallica's "Welcome Home (Sanitarium)" (*Master of Puppets*,
1986) includes a recurring gesture that similarly recalls the song's swagger gesture. Vernon Reid (the African American rock guitarist, formerly
of Living Colour) also quoted the song's 7/4 instrumental section in one
of his songs. So, numerous, highly diverse filmmakers, TV creators, and
musicians have engaged with Rush's music. In addition, the song appears on numerous rock music anthologies. Also, the Los Angeles album-rock radio station KLOS has used the song's distinctive opening
synthesizer sound within its multiartist style-signifying collage. A late-
2000 Nissan Maxima TV ad used the same opening part of the song,
including the subsequent drumming. However, an excerpt from the
album's following song—about a car—might have been more appropriate.

"Red Barchetta"

Neil Peart found the inspiration for the album's second song, "Red
Barchetta" (6:10), in a 1973 short story (Foster 1973). The song's protagonist defies the "Motor Law" and races his uncle's vintage title car (a
kind of Ferrari) through the countryside. He gets into a high-speed
chase with the police (driving a "gleaming alloy air-car"); then the music
eases up as the narrator loses them and ends up back at his uncle's
country farmhouse. One can easily imagine late twentieth-century versions of Tom Sawyer and Huckleberry Finn taking a pristine sports car
out for a spin, just to see if they can get away with it. Arguably, John
Hughes accomplished this very feat in *Ferris Bueller's Day Off* (1986).
In that film, a trio of teenage misfits "borrow" a preserved sports car for
just such a joyride. In Rush's song, the car's "well-weathered leather,
hot metal and oil . . . the blur of the landscape" and its "screeching
tires" are fused with the song's rhythmic flow and fairly visceral feeling.

The song's music video also includes basic, early computer animation, similar to racing car video games of the early to mid-1980s.

"YYZ"

The third track on *Moving Pictures*, "YYZ" (pronounced, in Anglo-Canadian style, "YY Zed," 4:26) is Rush's best-known instrumental work. In keeping with the band's less extreme approach of the early 1980s, it lasts for less than half the duration of the band's preceding instrumental work, "La Villa Strangiato" (4:26 vs. 9:34). Among other things, the work keeps its synthesizer components and "odd time signatures" relatively modest and, most importantly, balances alternations among unison (everyone playing together), contrapuntal (polyphonic or "multi-voiced"), and homophonic ("chordal") textures. The U.S. Academy of Recording Arts and Sciences recognized the song's broad "musicianly" appeal by nominating it for the 1981 Grammy for Best Rock Instrumental. However, "YYZ" lost to another rock trio—the Police's post-progressive, post-punk, modal, semiexotic, and minimalism-inspired "Behind My Camel" (*Zenyatta Mondatta*, 1980).

Rush often used unusual time signatures and complex rhythms in order to make a point or sometimes just to "mix things up." The band bases the opening of "YYZ" on Morse code for the radio call letters of Toronto's main airport: Pearson International. Many Rush fans collect "YYZ" baggage tags. Canadian airports use identifiers based on weather transmitter codes, not on city names.

Y -.- - Y -.- - Z - -.. or 7/8 + 7/8 + 3/4 or q e q q q e q q q q e e or 5/4 x 2

Peart first sounds the Morse code pattern on the bell of his ride cymbal (0:00–0:05), and that unusual initial sound thus gives the effect of a radio signal. The band then transforms the pattern musically (0:05–0:29). Lifeson alternates the two pitches of a low tritone (a highly dissonant interval) on quarter notes and eighth notes. (This recalls the main theme of "La Villa Strangiato.") Lee plays a slow-moving synthesizer line that meanders from the tritone's one pitch to the other. Rush performed "YYZ" in concert well over a thousand times between 1981 and 2013. Thus, it provided the band with a kind of perpetual connection to its home city.

After the opening sections, a brief, "sputtering" passage (with Lee on bass, 0:29–0:36) functions as a transition to the next section, which features virtuosic 12/8 unison embellishments of the dissonant tritone (0:36–0:43). The following music (0:43–1:11 and 1:11–1:38) provides a playful two-part 4/4 section, first with the guitar and bass in unison and then in elaborate counterpoint. Some of this section recalls stylistic features of early-1970s progressive rock, especially music by the UK band Yes. The following section features Lifeson's funky, syncopated guitar chords alternating with highly virtuosic "stop-time" interjections by Lee on bass and by Peart on drums (1:38–2:22). Lifeson then plays a semivirtuosic guitar solo over the still-continuing changes (2:22–2:51), with Peart adding unusual, sample-like sounds.

After the guitar solo, which ends with an unaccompanied descending sequence (as in Vivaldi's violin music), a slower, 2/2 section with a pedal in the bass and brassy synthesizer chords (2:51–3:20) provides what Neil Peart calls the "big sappy . . . bridge in the middle that is really orchestrated, really emotional, really rich [to] half symboli[ze] the tremendous emotional impact of coming home" (Banasiewicz 1988, 54). After the bridge, the band reprises the unison and contrapuntal "playful elaboration" sections (0:43–1:11–1:38) at 3:20–3:48–4:14. A final virtuosic pairing of bass and drums (4:14–4:17) leads into a brief Morse code tritone coda (4:17–4:26). On the whole, the work evokes mechanical signals followed by complicated hesitancies, the excitement of traveling somewhere new, and a new set of signals at the end. This affirms Peart's comments that "the song is loosely based on airport-associated images. Exotic destinations, painful partings, happy landings, that sort of thing" ("The Drummer Sounds Off" 1990). Peart elsewhere explains that this provided a "shorter, more concise instrumental that was actually a song with verses and a chorus . . . à la [jazz-rock band] Weather Report" (Banasiewicz 1988, 54).

"Limelight"

The first half of *Moving Pictures* concludes with "Limelight" (4:19), the album's fourth song. As its title suggests, the song concerns fame, but Peart's lyrics actually incorporate *both* meanings of "limelight." (The concert stages on which Rush regularly performed for thousands of fans featured extensive lighting systems.) In his lyrics, Peart outlines a quite personal perspective and admits to a certain degree of discomfort about public life, which would have included constant autograph seekers and a continual lack of personal space. He is painfully shy, for a "rock star." Several earlier Rush songs provide precedents for these lyrics. For example, "Making Memories" (*Fly by Night*, 1975) outlines the band's positive attitude about its touring apprenticeship ("We go on diggin' every show"). However, it also accepts the transitory nature of the music business ("[In] the morning . . . it's time for us to go").

Musically, "Limelight" features an energetic, distorted guitar riff, but the song's frequent meter shifts also underscore the discomfort and mixed feelings experienced by the protagonist, and the song ends in the resigned-sounding relative minor. In 1988, music journalist Robin Tolleson introduced jazz drummer (and former Miles Davis associate) Tony Williams to "Limelight." Williams spontaneously provided a sense of the song's "feel" or "groove":

> Even though it's a 7/4 here and goes into 3 over there, it feels really relaxed. I get an emotional feeling from it. I like the bass playing and the bass sound. The groove is good, and that's the bass and the drums. (Tolleson 1988)

On Rush's ongoing use of such time signatures, Geddy Lee points out:

> We've played in seven almost as much as we've played in 4/4, you know. So for us to be into seven is the most natural thing in the world. It's probably as natural to us as it is for Bill Bruford [of Yes, King Crimson, etc.] to play in five. He can make it seem so smooth. . . . But it depends on how familiar you are with that particular feel and how much you thought out the music . . . so it doesn't feel herky-jerky. (Mulhern 1986, 86)

In "Limelight," the band certainly demonstrates the influence of earlier progressive rock in its complex rhythms. However, the song also recalls Rush's earlier "Something for Nothing" (1976) and "Circumstances" (1978), with Lifeson's riffs and guitar solo thus evoking heavy metal.

There are various cover versions of "Limelight," including one by Canadian singer-songwriter and guitarist Jacob Moon (live looping, etc., pop-rock, *Fascination*, 2013). Much of the song was also used for the opening sequence of the episode "Rock Night" on April 3, 2013, for television's *American Idol*, although no Rush song appears to have been played by any of the episode's performers. Album-rock radio stations frequently play this song, and it also appears on some rock anthologies, including Rhino Records' anthology of 1980s power rock (2000).

The Rest of *Moving Pictures*

The opening song of the second half of *Moving Pictures*, "The Camera Eye" (11:58), comprises Rush's last composition with a duration of more than 7:31. Influenced by the early twentieth-century U.S. author John Dos Passos (e.g., vivid characterizations and point-blank stream-of-consciousness writing), the song evokes images of New York and then London. After opening city sounds (e.g., car horns, cars, police whistles, yelling), it begins with a multisectional instrumental introduction, thus recalling the openings of "Xanadu" and "Cygnus X-1" (1977). The song initially features Lee's array of synthesizers, and he abandons his bass guitar in favour of these "electro-pop" elements for about the first half of the song. Various parallel musical features (recalling aspects of "Hemispheres") underscore a verse for each of New York and London, including a shuffle between 3/4 and 6/8 rhythms (recalling Leonard Bernstein's "America" from *West Side Story*) and a wavering 4/4 bridge that suggests the influence of Jamaican ska music. Both cities get the same chorus: "I feel the sense of possibilities. I feel the wrench of hard realities. The focus is sharp in the city." The song ends with fading synthesizer and guitar sounds and the distant sounds of Big Ben. (Rush earlier referenced Big Ben in "Xanadu.")

The second-last song on *Moving Pictures*, "Witch Hunt" (sixth) presents a gloomy, small-scale version of Arthur Miller's play *The Crucible* (1953). In fact, my high school production of *The Crucible* (in which I played Reverend Parris) used this song as part of its intermission music. The song updates Miller's McCarthy-era "witch hunt" morality tale to treat the potential ongoing strangeness of immigrants, infidels, theater, and literature. It portrays the ignorant and self-righteous with slow, "evil-sounding" tritones (compared to the fast ones in "YYZ") and rhetorically applied, uneasy-sounding alternations among its various time signatures (compared to the smooth ones in "Limelight"). Hugh Syme also plays keyboards on this song, and the opening includes drunken, indistinct "preachy" voices. Peart wrote this song as part 3, though the first appearing, of a series of lyrics called "Fear." During its 1984 tour, the band played the recently completed "Fear" trilogy: "The Enemy Within," "The Weapon," and "Witch Hunt." Rush tribute bands, including one I heard in the summer of 2001, also later played them in this "reverse" order.

The album's seventh and final song, "Vital Signs," provides a window into the band's willingness to incorporate technology beyond the occasional synthesized pedal point, semiexperimental song introduction, and instrumental "middle." The song also features a prominent, ska-like backbeat in many of its sections. This recalls certain elements in the same album's "The Camera Eye" and the application of a kind of reggae style in "The Spirit of Radio" (1980). Additionally, the lyrics seem to favor renewal, and the song feels like Rush wrote and recorded it very quickly. For example, they did not correct Lee's substitution, presumably accidental, of the nonword "evelate" for the word "elevate" in part of the song. The song features synthesizers as rivals to the electric guitar in the song's structural and textural underpinning. Despite the frequent use of synthesizers on *Moving Pictures*, at the time Lee said, "I still don't consider myself a keyboard player—maybe a synthesist" ("Geddy Lee/Rush" 1981).

Rush's second live album (*Exit . . . Stage Left*, late 1981, recorded in Canada and the UK) appeared before the band completed any new studio material. "The Trees" (1978) includes a classical guitar introduction called "Broon's Bane." Hugh Syme's cover includes elements of all the preceding Rush album covers, and the album title recalls the catchphrase of Hanna-Barbera's TV cartoon character Snagglepuss. Presumably, a visual representation of the character would have required elaborate (and expensive) legal undertakings. Its opening acts of the early 1980s included Canadian progressive- or blues-oriented artists FM, Pat Travers, Max Webster, and Saga, plus UK heavy metal group Saxon and U.S. hard rock group .38 Special. However, the band itself then mainly continued with its enthusiasm for synthesizers and similar music technology on its subsequent four studio albums (1982–1987).

5

"BE COOL OR BE CAST OUT"

Fusions with Synth Rock and New Wave, 1982–1984

After its success with *Moving Pictures* (1981), Rush quickly released its second live album (*Exit . . . Stage Left*, 1981, recorded in Canada and the UK) and its ninth and tenth studio albums (*Signals*, 1982, and *Grace under Pressure*, 1984). People who became Rush fans within different chronological periods have quite differing opinions as to when Rush became the most mainstream. However, various musical and contextual factors (album sales, spin-offs, etc.) strongly suggest that the period from 1980 to 1984 witnessed Rush's most significant diffusion into "normal" musical culture.

MAINSTREAM ADJACENCY

Signals includes the band's ode to suburbia: the progressive synth-rock song "Subdivisions"—as well as the band's only U.S. Top 40 hit: the synth-pop- and new-wave-influenced "New World Man." In 1981, Geddy Lee had also provided the vocals for the Bob and Doug McKenzie ("SCTV") comedy song "Take Off [to the Great White North]," which actually charted higher in the United States (No. 16) than "New World Man" (No. 21). "Take Off" appears on Rhino Records' seven-CD compilation *Like Omigod! The '80s Popular Culture Box (Totally)*. *Grace under Pressure* includes such FM radio "album tracks" as "Distant Early Warning" (also one of the band's best videos), "Afterimage," and "Red Sector A."

In the period from 1982 to 1984, Rush frequently began to use synthesizers, samplers, and electronic percussion. The band also distilled its 1970s-style progressive eccentricities into the instrumental middle sections of its songs. Peart's lyrical ideas came to include alienation and fear, science and technology, non-Western influences, NASA, and the late Cold War.

MUSIC TECHNOLOGY ASSUMES CONTROL, 1982–1984

From 1969 to 1981, many technologically inclined persons gravitated toward the intricacies and power of progressive rock, hard rock, and heavy metal. Rush often focused on the technique, virtuosity, song structures, and rhythmic complexities of progressive rock. Normally, the band combined these approaches with hard rock or heavy metal. However, around 1976–1978 the band also gradually began to use synthesizers and related performance technology. Not all Rush fans felt that this was a good idea.

From 1976 to 1981, Rush sometimes used keyboard and foot-pedal synthesizers, but five of the six songs on *Permanent Waves* (1980) and all seven on *Moving Pictures* (1981) use some synthesizers, such as an Oberheim OB-X and a Roland JP-8 (Jupiter). In 1976, Hugh Syme played an ARP Odyssey synthesizer on "2112" and a Mellotron 400 on "Tears." In 1980, Syme played piano on "The Spirit of Radio" and "Different Strings." In 1977–1978, Geddy Lee himself sometimes played a monophonic Minimoog synthesizer or Moog Taurus pedals for certain melodies or pedal points, and the band discarded the idea of hiring an onstage keyboardist. Lee took piano lessons (as well as singing as a choral boy soprano) as a child in Toronto, received informal keyboard instruction for *A Farewell to Kings* (1977), and resumed piano lessons in the mid-1980s. "Hemispheres" (1978) includes Lee's first recorded use of a polyphonic synthesizer (an Oberheim), and a related module also sometimes interfaced with a Taurus pedal unit. As microcomputers then began to flourish in the early 1980s, so did digital synthesizers, melodic sequencers, and electronic percussion. In that period, Rush produced its most "technological" albums: *Signals* (1982),

Grace under Pressure (1984), *Power Windows* (1985), and *Hold Your Fire* (1987). A few of Peart's lyrics addressed technology, but Rush's use of certain instruments did so to a much greater extent.

From 1982 to 1988, in addition to his bass guitars, Lee used as many as five keyboards onstage (from among a Minimoog, Oberheim OB-Xa, Roland Jupiter JP-8, PPG Wave 2.2 or 2.3 with Waveterm digital sampling unit, Emulator II, Yamaha DX-7, Roland D-50, Prophet VS, and Yamaha KX-76 controller), two pedal systems (Moog Taurus I and/or II and later a Korg MIDI unit), and two melodic and/or rhythmic sequencers (Oberheim DSX, Roland TR-808, and/or Yamaha QX-1). By 1985, in addition to various guitars, even Lifeson used a pair of bass pedal units, two offstage Emulator II sampling keyboards, and a digital sequencer. In addition to his early-1980s effects (MXR, Delta Lab, Roland, Yamaha, etc.), he added numerous ones in 1985 (Loft, Ibanez, Boss, Scholz-Rockman, etc.).

For certain songs around 1984–1988, Neil Peart wore headphones in concert so that his drumming could match the tempos of electronically generated sequences and arpeggios. He wears such headphones in the video for "Red Sector A," which further suggests that the band wished to "play up" the high-tech nature of its music in the 1980s. The visual artists filmed the video for this song on a Rush concert stage (as they did for certain earlier Rush videos), but they also incorporated shots from actual concerts, including flash-pot explosions and fan reactions. Peart's varied/extensive drumming approach sometimes involved Simmons electronic drums (as in 1984's "Red Sector A," 1985's "Mystic Rhythms," and others), samplers, and other electronic equipment. On tour, he combined his 1982 Tama Artstar prototype drums (plus Avedis Zildjian cymbals, etc.) with a satellite set largely involving electronics. In this period, Peart and his drum technicians began to place his drums on a rotating platform so he could face forward in any of several configurations. (He used similar platform technology for his drum solos on later tours, especially in the 2000s.) In 1987–1988, he replaced his glockenspiel with a KAT electronic MIDI mallet unit. He also used dedicated Akai sampling modules and various additional electronic triggers.

SIGNALS (1982)

Hugh Syme's cover for *Signals* shows a Dalmatian sniffing a red fire hydrant. This implies fire services at one level but the dog's basic physiological needs at another. (The hydrant "signals" the dog to urinate on it.) The pristine lawn reflects a well-maintained suburban yard. The back cover shows a fictitious subdivision with Rush-related names, such as Olde Dirk Road, Lerxtwood Mall, and a firm named Pratt & Associates (based on Lee, Lifeson, and Peart's band nicknames, respectively). The neighborhood also includes a baseball joke, Line Drive, based on Geddy Lee's appreciation for that sport. The songs "Subdivisions" and "The Analog Kid" presumably inspired the suburban imagery. The band again recorded the album at Le Studio in Quebec, coproducing it with Terry Brown and recording it with engineer Paul Northfield. Shortly after the album's release, Peart said:

> I guess that *Signals* has more to do with writing about people and less about ideals. . . . I'm trying to make . . . symbols into real people and real conflicts in real people's lives. I still want to write about ideals. I'm not interested in writing about the sewer of life. (Makowski 1982)

In other words, *Signals* often concerns various types of communication.

"Subdivisions"

The opening track of Rush's *Signals* (1982), "Subdivisions," uses brassy, square-wave synthesizer patterns almost constantly throughout. No earlier Rush song had used a synthesizer to this extent, and Lifeson's guitar can barely be heard apart from a brief solo (4:18–4:39) that follows Lee's second synthesizer solo (3:57–4:18). Lee wrote the entire song on a keyboard, and he especially makes use of the wide frequency range and organic punch of his Roland analog (JP-8, "Jupiter") synthesizer. In an interesting development in the 2000s, Canadian singer-songwriter and guitarist Jacob Moon created a well-received and Rush-approved cover version (and video) of "Subdivisions" that instrumentally uses *only* guitar sounds—including live looping (live, *The Loop*, 2008).

    The technological direction of *Signals* resulted in Lee's own historical confusion over this album, calling it "definitely the direction that we've wanted to go" in 1982 (Makowski 1982), "confusing" in 1984 (Oliver 1984), and "a failure in getting the right balance" in 1991 (Schulte 1991). The later comments suggest that Lee wished to apologize for the shortcomings of *Signals*, especially the analog synthesizer "punch" that often buried Lifeson's guitar. Although continuing to explore music technology, the band successfully redressed that balance between 1984 and 1987. Although more modest in scope than some of the band's earlier work, "Subdivisions" still addresses relatively serious issues, and in addition to "common" 4/4 time it also makes substantial use of 3/4 and 7/8.

The song engages extensively with synthesizer technology, but its lyrics do not really have to do with technology. Instead, it concerns restless young persons, especially "dreamers and misfits," who want to escape from suburbia, which "sprawl[s] on the fringes of the city . . . in between the bright lights and the far unlit unknown." The "Subdivisions" video shows a teenage male playing video games, walking around downtown Toronto, being teased by cooler high school students, and watching a video of Rush performing this song—just as an annoyed parent tosses him his homework. Peart's lyrics, however, acknowledge the irony that the ones who escape from the suburbs and head for the city often long for the suburbs later in life—"somewhere to relax their restless flight, somewhere out of a memory of lighted streets on quiet nights."

"Subdivisions" partly conforms to Rush's trademark "progressive" 7/8 time signature, as in the beginning of the song's introduction. Also, the middle portion of each half verse switches from 4/4 to 7/8, so that change happens four times during the song. The rhythmic shift underscores lyrics about the suburbs' "geometric order, [functioning as] an insulated border in between [city and country]," with its "opinions all provided . . . the future predecided . . . detached and subdivided." Later, the same metrical shift inscribes the cities' "timeless old attraction," with individuals "cruising for the action" and "lit up like a firefly" at night, but losing "the race to rats," getting "caught in ticking traps," and, ironically, starting to dream of the suburbs. The parallel recalls the band's use of identical music to represent Apollo and Dionysus in 1978's "Hemispheres" and London and New York in 1981's "The Camera Eye." The song's title references the suburban subdivisions with which the song concerns itself lyrically (and in the video), but it also references the metrical subdivisions that musically underscore verse 1's dislike of the suburbs *and* verse 2's ambivalence about having left them. In beginning to use music technology so extensively, Lee probably recognized an ironic parallel of Peart's urban "ticking traps."

The Rest of *Signals*

"The Analog Kid" (second) features a lyrical theme somewhat similar to that of "Subdivisions." Lifeson's guitar plays a more prominent role, and the song inscribes a fast, backbeat-driven 4/4. This slows to cut-time for the chorus and solo sections. In the chorus, a voice-like synthesizer patch provides a "bright and nameless vision['s] . . . call" of places and experiences other than those of one's small town or suburban home. Peart later pointed to "The Analog Kid" as his "first attempt at nonfiction" and suggested that by 1982 he had sufficient "confidence and technique" to "step outside" of his characters instead of "stepping inside" them (Krewen 1990, 37).

The third song, "Chemistry," mainly follows a dance-like moderate 4/4, but with numerous textural shifts. Most of the song's instrumental sections use polyphonic synthesizer chords, active drums, occasionally circular guitar gestures, and, often, Moog Taurus pedals instead of bass guitar. Lee reports that he wrote this song on keyboards (Armbruster 1984, 60). The "synth pop" chorus features a voice-like monophonic synthesizer line, active drums, somewhat active bass, and, apart from a solo, considerably less guitar than in the keyboard-less, hard rock verses. The song's lyrics (credited to all three band members) and its textural shifts explore the band's chemistry in combining electricity (i.e., synthesizers) and biology (i.e., traditional rock music instruments).

"Digital Man" (fourth) ironically makes comparatively little use of synthesizers. The verses use power chords with virtuosic drums and bass and suggest that the central character functions as a futuristic information collector. The bridge uses reggae-influenced backbeats and textural/chorused rhythm and blues guitar and sees the protagonist wishing to retire from "Babylon" to a tropical island: "Zion" or "Avalon." (Those references suggest further Jamaican influences.) The brief chorus section uses a prominent synthesizer part: a thumpy, mechanical, bass-guitar replacement. This reveals that the digital man "won't need a bed" because he is an android. The character is also said to be "adept at adaptation."

The fifth song, "The Weapon," begins by paraphrasing U.S. president Franklin D. Roosevelt's famous 1933 statement about socioeconomic fear in the Great Depression: "The only thing we have to fear is fear itself." Peart transforms the declarative statement into a rhetorical question in order to address its renewed (or continuing) relevance, and he follows this with several similar constructions: "We've got nothing to fear—but fear itself? Not pain or failure, not fatal tragedy? Not the faulty units in this mad machinery? Not the broken contacts in emotional chemistry?" Peart wrote the song's lyrics as part 2 of "Fear," and he addresses his ideological fear that so many of his fellow humans let religious movements and governments keep them in a blissful ignorance. Following "Witch Hunt" (part 3, 1981), "Fear" continues with "The Enemy Within" (part 1, 1984) and "Freeze" (part 4, 2002). Lee wrote the song on keyboards, and he used an electronic arpeggiator for some of its hypnotic synthesizer elements.

Rush wrote and recorded its only U.S. Top 40 hit, "New World Man" (No. 21), the album's sixth song, in a few hours. Revealingly, the song avoids such progressive hard rock features as odd time signatures, a guitar solo, and elaborate instrumental (e.g., unison) sections. It begins with a simple, diatonic, synth pop synthesizer pattern. The timbre changes (i.e., flanges) slightly on each of the pattern's consecutive eighth notes, and the pattern also underlies the song's verses, but at a much more subtle volume level. Interlocking drum, bass, and guitar patterns join in and accompany the song's first verse. The first part of the lyrics concerns a "restless young romantic," "a rebel and a runner" who "wants to run the big machine." Relatively active drums and bass, reggae-influenced (backbeat) guitar chords, and a slow-moving synthesizer line (incorporating filter sweeps) accompany the bridge, which espouses the combination of "old world" and "third world" tendencies. Not surprisingly, the song combines 1970s British rock with 1980s "world beat" rhythmic influences. The chorus then establishes a hard rock/guitar-based riff. This suggests that the band wished to make its "own mistakes" and to accept that "constant change is here today." The end of each chorus provides the earliest instances (after Rush's 1973 single) of Lee providing his own vocal harmonies, something he gradually increased over the following two decades—culminating in his solo album (*My Favourite Headache*, 2000) and Rush's next several studio albums (2002–2012).

The seventh (second-last) song, "Losing It," tells the stories of aging artists steeped in self-doubt: a dancer and a writer modeled on Ernest Hemingway. As Peart explains: "As a writer Hemingway thought that the most important thing was to sustain a reputation and integrity. Hopefully, all of the other fruits would follow from that. And for us as a band, myself as a musician, that was the idealistic goal with which we started out" (Krewen 1986, 8). In the song and in interviews, Peart avoids specific information about Hemingway's actual outcome: suicide by shotgun after undergoing a series of electroshock treatments for clinical depression and other ailments. Nevertheless, the song inscribes melancholy. Ben Mink's guest contributions on electric violin provide an emotional depth that inspired the band to pursue similar real-life topics between 1984 and 2002. Hemingway surfaces a number of times in a number of different ways in Rush's music as well as in Peart's "extracurricular" interests in physical challenges (e.g., cycling).

The eighth and final song on *Signals*, "Countdown," bridges the band's enthusiasm for general technology with its use of music technology. Like "Subdivisions," the song contains a high degree of synthesizers, and like "New World Man" it includes no guitar solo. The song recounts the band's attendance as VIP guests at NASA's inaugural space shuttle (*Columbia*) launch on April 12, 1981. Ayn Rand similarly attended the 1969 Apollo 11 launch as a VIP guest and similarly enthused about the event as evidence of man's "grandeur":

> One knew that this spectacle was not the product of inanimate nature, like some aurora borealis, or of chance, or of luck, that it was unmistakably human—with "human," for once, meaning grandeur—that a purpose and a long, sustained, disciplined effort had gone to achieve this series of moments, and that man was succeeding. For once, if only for seven minutes, the worst among those who saw it had to feel—not "How small is man by the side of the Grand Canyon!"—but "How great is man and how safe is nature when he conquers it!" (Rand 1969, 6)

In the same article, Rand complains (pp. 10–12) about "humanities"/"collectivist" intellectuals and media commentators. Most such persons either didn't care about the "rationalist triumph" of Apollo 11 or else made it clear that earthbound social issues should have been the priority of the day. In fact, Rand holds (p. 8) that the U.S. government should not have spent so much money on an enormous project that would have come about through laissez-faire principles of capitalism.

"Countdown" uses brassy synthesizer patterns that recall the album's opening song, "Subdivisions." It also uses numerous tape-recorded samples of the actual *Columbia* launch activities, including the sounds of helicopters, the voices of mission control, the *Columbia* astronauts, and the launch itself. Peart bases much of his percussion on snare drum rolls, thus sounding "military." The music builds, in order to underscore the excitement of such an occasion. At certain points among the audio samples of the narrative—for example, launch ignition and leaving Earth's atmosphere—the rhythms alternate between 6/4 and 7/8 (2:54–3:09 and, for the fade-out, 5:00–5:50). This adds to the excitement of this "leading edge" application of technology. Lifeson says of the metrical complexities:

> It's more of a feel thing than a conscious effort. The way we write, we have the lyric or an idea of what the song is going to be. That idea sets a mood. By changing the time signature you can change the whole effect of the song. (Lifeson 1984)

The song's "feel" or "effect"—excitement, danger—hinges on those changes. Music must have been played at some point surrounding the launch, because we hear mission control and the astronauts (Young and Crippen) expressing their appreciation for it near the end of the song. Possibly, Rush provided their NASA VIP acquaintances with recordings of some of its earlier music, but in any case only a few later Rush songs integrate general technology and music technology as closely as "Countdown."

GRACE UNDER PRESSURE (1984)

In a controversial move, Rush abandoned its longtime associate Terry ("Broon") Brown and engaged former Supertramp producer Peter Henderson to coproduce its 1984 album, *Grace under Pressure*. The band wanted a change in producer, but its desire for a renewed balance in technology and coproduction resulted in a difficult recording period.

The band took three months to write the album and five months to record it, again at Le Studio in Quebec. The recording of the vocal tracks for the opening song, "Distant Early Warning," alone took ten hours to complete. The album title, its inner photo of an egg precariously lodged in a C-clamp, and Hugh Syme's cover art reflect the stylistic difficulties of this period. In addition, the internationally renowned Canadian portrait photographer Yousuf Karsh (1908–2002) took the band's photo for this album. Most famous for his World War II photograph of a grumpy Winston Churchill, Karsh had never before photographed a rock band. On the album cover, an android observes a circuit board (?) suspended between ominous storm clouds (pressure, abbreviated "p") and a shimmering oceanic liquid (grace or "g").

"Distant Early Warning"

The song and video for "Distant Early Warning" (the album's opening song) update the earlier years of the Cold War to the height of the late Cold War and the conservative era (Thatcher, Reagan, etc.) of twenty years later. The video was directed by David Mallet, who filmed it in front of an "artsy" map of the world. The concept borrows from Stanley Kubrick's film *Dr. Strangelove; or, How I Learned to Stop Worrying and Love the Bomb* (1964). The imagery includes flight controls, a bomber, a melting-wax mock-up of Lee's face, and a young boy (who is *not* Geddy Lee's son) "riding" the bomb over nature and cities. The set is moderately high tech: Lee plays a compact Steinberger bass, although he actually wrote the song on a keyboard. Peart's Simmons electronic drums appear prominently, although he mainly uses his red acoustic Tama set in this song. By 1984, he had come to accept electronic drums, and his particular combination of drums and cymbals with electronic drums could thus be called "electro-acoustic."

The song's instrumental introduction includes the sounds of static, suggesting radiation or perhaps a Geiger counter measuring it. Peart's opening words support an interpretation involving a concern for nature about the threat of nuclear annihilation: "There's no swimming in the heavy water, no singing in the acid rain." However, he also incorporates the difficulty of human relationships and puns on obsolete, absolute, and Absalom. This last word simultaneously references William Faulkner's novel *Absalom, Absalom!* (1936) and the biblical story of King

David's grief over the death of his son Absalom. In part of his solo (3:15–3:28), Lifeson uses a Delta Lab Harmonicomputer to play in octaves.

The band plays the song's main instrumental hook (initially at 0:28–0:39) in 7/8 with some 5/8. Lee uses keyboards and bass pedals for that section. In addition to stressing the asymmetrical rhythms, the song's main hook seems to wish to force one particular, unusual mode, whereas other parts of the song favor several further ones. By pairing the "old Rush" rhythms with Lee's "new Rush" synthesizers, the mode of the song's main hook also suggests an enthusiasm for technology. The other modes, though, suggest a comparatively pessimistic view concerning the survival both of nature and of human relationships in a complex world.

"Afterimage"

Lee wrote the album's second song, "Afterimage," on keyboards. Peart's lyrics concern a friend and band-related colleague, Robbie Whelan, who had died in a car accident. (The band dedicated the album "In memory of Robbie Whelan.") The song, however, can't quite decide if it wants to remember happier times with him or just mourn his loss. The word "afterimage" refers to the mental effect of still seeing something even though it no longer remains in your field of vision. By choosing this title, Peart reasonably suggests that this parallels remembering a friend, and Peart completed the lyrics before any of the music was written—which was somewhat unusual for Rush. The song's verses use a simple, minor mode, but balanced with almost "snappy" rhythms. The choruses, though, sound comparatively negative and have more complex chords, slower/resigned rhythms, and a kind of blues-inspired call-and-response. The song ends in a tonally negative-sounding way. Over a decade later, Neil Peart's daughter Selena Taylor died in a car crash (in 1997) and his spouse Jacqueline Taylor then died of cancer (in 1998). The band dedicated its 1998 live album, *Different Stages*, "In loving memory of Jackie and Selena" and also included in the liner notes the opening lines of "Afterimage": "Suddenly . . . you were gone . . . from all the lives you left your mark upon."

"Red Sector A"

Peart named the album's third song, "Red Sector A," after the shuttle launch area the band visited for NASA's shuttle launch in the spring of 1981, which also inspired Rush's 1982 song "Countdown." However, the lyrics of "Red Sector A" actually concern a wartime, concentration camp scenario in which a young man has lost his father and brother and hopes that he can rise to the challenge of seeing his mother through the rest of the ordeal. This originated in Peart reading the accounts of war survivors, but he frames the lyrics just generically enough that they can refer to the prisoners of any war and also to slavery. Lee's parents survived the concentration camps at Auschwitz, and Peart may have wished to write something more personal for Lee to sing.

Peart's drumming, which never pauses, suggests dance-pop and features metronomic closed hi-hat eighth notes, disorienting open hi-hat and other sounds, and, nearly half of the time, at least some of the sounds (especially tom-tom fills), on Simmons electronic drums. Lifeson uses a whammy bar to make the song's opening chords seem somehow ungrounded, and one of the earliest portions of his guitar solo (ca. 3:09–3:18) provides exotic-sounding sevenths by means of electronically derived harmonics generated on a Harmonicomputer. These provide familiar-yet-exotic sentiments to parallel Peart's lyrics. Lee uses an electronic arpeggiator for some of the more hypnotic synthesizer elements. Most revealing, though, Lee does not play a bass guitar at any point during this song, not even for the short periods when he does not play keyboards and not for the song's filmed-onstage video. Thus, synthesized elements participate without pause. Also, the song remains in 4/4 time, and it contains no overt "progressive" melodic/rhythmic unison or contrapuntal passages.

The video for "Red Sector A" shows four synthesizers and Moog Taurus II pedals on Geddy Lee's part of the stage. In the same period, Alex Lifeson also sometimes used Moog Taurus I pedals and made substantial use of his Stratocaster's whammy bar (vibrato arm) for atmospheric guitar effects inspired by recent post-punk and new wave rock music.

The Rest of *Grace under Pressure*

Peart wrote the lyrics for the fourth song, "The Enemy Within," as part 1 of "Fear." He wrote the three song lyrics in reverse order, becoming the most personal by part 1. This installment involves a psychological fear of things outside resulting in keeping one's ambition bottled up inside. (The unanticipated part 4, "Freeze," appeared in 2002.) The tempo holds back slightly and the rhythms seem inspired by ska in the verses, with Lifeson providing slower offbeat chords. The chorus and the bridge use hard rock style, but the postchorus instrumental section, after the words "experience to extremes," uses an airy synth pop sound. The song begins with the hard rock style, before establishing the ska verse. By comparison, the song ends with ska, but with hard rock rhythms *and* keyboards.

Walt Whitman's "I Sing the Body Electric" from *Leaves of Grass* (1855 edition) enthuses about the physiology of the human body, and Neil Peart used this as his lyrical starting point for "The Body Electric," the album's fifth song. In some ways, though, the song more closely recalls *Star Wars* creator George Lucas's early film *THX 1138* (1971). The song's lyrics refer to a "humanoid escapee," an "android on the run . . . trying to change its program." The computer imagery expands to "data overload," "memory banks unloading . . . bytes break[ing] into bits," and, especially, to the binary code sung during the chorus (and related drum pattern): "1-0-0-1-0-0-1." The paranoid and panicky situation of the song's lyrics recall Lucas's film through words such as: "S.O.S.," "in distress," "trouble," "break down," "struggle," "resist," "a pulse of dying power," "a hundred years of routines," and "pray[ing] to the mother of all machines."

The song's rhythms remain suitably off kilter and avoid the obvious 4/4 downbeats. The tempo remains quite fast, which is particularly odd given the deliberately dour pacing of Lucas's film. After the initial drums/bass/guitar groove, Lee prominently uses synthesizers, although he often pairs the keyboard sounds with his contributions on bass guitar. The synthesizers provide voice-like or "crystalline" timbres, via a recently acquired PPG digital synthesizer, played via a melodic sequencer or foot pedals. The keyboard parts support the central rhythms up into the higher frequencies, and the approach also corrects one of the most common complaints about *Signals* (1982): that the keyboard-oriented songs on that album often diminished, or at least substantially veiled, the band's traditional instrumental interplay. On the other hand, the song's guitar solo features *only* guitar, bass, and drums, in a highly contrapuntal ("traditional Rush") texture. Overcoming these sorts of "balance challenges" resulted in the album's title: *Grace under Pressure*, which derives from the definition of "guts" that Ernest Hemingway provided to Dorothy Parker in an interview in 1929.

The album's sixth song, "Kid Gloves," begins with a delay-effected guitar, weak (inverted) chords, subtle drums, and a basic keyboard line, which continue into verse 1. The lyrics mention being overwhelmed and out of touch, which is also inscribed by the verses' 5/4 time signature, the music's gentle resignation, and Lee's lower singing range (musical "kid gloves"?). The bridge switches quite drastically to 4/4, power chords, no synthesizer, slightly higher vocals, and lyrics about frustration and anger. The end of bridge 2, on the words "tough to be so cool" (and additionally, on its reprise) provides an early instance (following "New World Man" and "Distant Early Warning") of Lee providing his own vocal harmonies. The instrumental section mostly comprises Lifeson's guitar solo, including a modest, inventive combination of whammy bar effects, harmonics, offbeat gestures, and strange parallel harmonies.

The seventh song, "Red Lenses," somewhat returns to the late–Cold War and nature themes of "Distant Early Warning." Peart puns on "red" and "read" (past tense) thus implicating the media in hyping only selected things about international relations and other issues of the day. The song implicates the semifictitious *National Midnight Star*, in turning people into what they believe (trash?). Ironically, the *National Midnight Star*, which for several years served as the premier Rush discussion group (and related website), degenerated into just such tabloid-like trash by the late 1990s. The song's lyrics vaguely address the disparity of global wealth versus poverty, and Peart uses a wide variety of red-related images ("red lenses") throughout the song. These include heartbeats, rising sun, battle, passion, Mars, dancing shoes, the Soviet Union, heat, and pain. The song's extremes in vocal range, tonality, and music technology underscore its view that the apparent black-and-white extremes within culture merely reinforce one another.

The eighth and final song, "Between the Wheels," builds largely upon Lee's brassy, offbeat two-chord synthesizer riff: from a dissonant to a weakly resolved chord. The harsh/unstable nature of the keyboard riff inspired the song's lyrics, with verses about living "between a rock and a hard place." Cultural aspects such as TV, war, uneasy streets, and "real time" make us dizzy. However, the riff's simplicity also gave Lifeson ample opportunity to contribute guitar parts. The song's bridge aborts the keyboards, and Lee's active bass and Peart's active drumming contrast Lifeson's atmospheric guitar chords. The lyrics of the bridge describe speeding through life, using the imagery of driving a fast car and of the wheels of time. Lee switches back to keyboards and bass pedals for the chorus, which clarifies the disparity between the mobility of "wheels" and the potential self-destructiveness of letting fast-moving time get the better of you. The lyrics of the chorus reference not only the "Star-Spangled Banner" and the 1932 Depression-era Bing Crosby hit "Brother, Can You Spare a Dime?" but also Ernest Hemingway's 1926 use of the phrase "lost generation" in *The Sun Also Rises* and T. S. Eliot's 1922 poem "The Wasteland." The song comments on the precarious Western world and transplants post–World War I/Depression-era ideas about moral loss and cultural aimlessness to the Cold War era.

Lee wrote the bass line of "Between the Wheels" with his left hand on a keyboard instead of on a bass guitar or bass pedals. Lee explains his self-conscious view of himself as a "keyboardist": "My actual ability on keyboards is somewhat limited, and I don't consider myself a keyboard player" (Armbruster 1984, 63–65). Lee first incorporated synthesizer melodies in 1977, but by 1982–1984 he composed a number of new songs *entirely* on keyboards.

In the late 1970s, 1980s, and early 1990s, Rush used a wide variety of technology onstage. The band members played, or at least triggered, virtually all keyboard and sequencer passages. By introducing bass pedal units, synthesizers, sequencers, arpeggiators, triggers, and samplers within its live performances between 1977 and 1988, Rush acknowledged the potential disparity of using recordings in live performance. The band chose to recreate its studio creations through a meticulous, noticeable application of such technology. Later, the band concerned itself less with this disparity. From 2002 to 2013, Lee included only one or two keyboards onstage, and he rarely played them. When the band played keyboard-heavy music from 1982 to 1987, it allowed offstage computers and samplers to play most of those sounds, and Lee focused mainly on bass and vocals. In addition, Lifeson only played guitar, even though he occasionally appeared to sing. Lee had sung nearly all the vocal overdubs (1984–2012) on the original recordings, and those were usually what one actually heard in live performances.

Lifeson worked on his guitar solos for "Afterimage," "Between the Wheels," and "Red Sector A" (the third song) apart from the rest of the songwriting process. He accomplished this mainly in his spare time at his home studio. He worked from basic early cassette demos of those songs made at Le Studio. Lifeson explains his mid-1980s views on fast playing and composed-out guitar solos:

> [A] whole Van Halen record of faster-than-lightning guitar playing is too much. . . . The most soul-wrenching kind of note, harmonic, or melodic solo passage that really moves and feels—that lives forever . . . I always remember how I felt when I went to see bands and the guitar player didn't play the same solo that he did on the record. I'd be going, "This is one of my favorite solos of all time. The guy's a bum!" . . . We do a lot of composites—taking bits of solos and putting them together. Then I relearn it, or if it slides in nicely from one section to the next, we keep it. (Lifeson 1984)

Lifeson disparages the flashy fastness and improvised live solos of other rock guitarists. Peart's move toward more emotional lyrics about nature, human nature, and other "real-world" topics largely explains Lifeson's desire for soul-wrenching guitar contributions that move or feel. He also indicates that he composed his mid-1980s guitar solos in much the same manner as the band composed its earlier extended works: putting separate bits together. Throughout the album, he uses a heavily chorused guitar sound and relatively spare chords and/or arpeggios. This resembles the playing of other 1980s guitarists, especially U2's "The Edge." An additional point of interest is that Kevin J. Anderson, a U.S. science-fiction author and eventual Neil Peart short-story collaborator, dedicated his novel *Resurrection Inc.* (1988) to the members of Rush. He borrowed certain ideas for the book from *Grace under Pressure*.

OTHER MUSICAL INFLUENCES ON RUSH, CIRCA 1984–1988

Geddy Lee refers to inspiration from the Fixx, Tears for Fears, Peter Gabriel (including synthesist Larry Fast and various drummers), Simple Minds, Ultravox, Talk Talk, Eurythmics, King Sunny Ade, Howard Jones, and King Crimson (i.e., their recent album *Three of a Perfect Pair*) (Armbruster 1984, 60–61). Much of this music makes prominent "post-progressive" use of synthesizers. Lee disdained the use by certain performers of remote (strap-on) keyboards as "too Vegas." In the mid-1980s, Lifeson mentioned his appreciation for the album *Win This Record* (1982) by the extremely eclectic California musician David Lindley (bluegrass, world beat, blues, rock and roll, etc.). Also, Lifeson's non-solo guitar contributions in Rush's music from 1984–1985 often resemble richly chorused, offbeat, horn/brass sections in a jazz or rhythm and blues band, thus also requiring an unusually broad definition of "progressive" to circumscribe Rush's music and influences.

Neil Peart mentioned growing up listening to big-band music and becoming inspired by the drummers who played with Glenn Miller, Duke Ellington, Count Basie, Frank Sinatra, and Tony Bennett. He pointed to the influence of Gene Krupa as well as to recent jazz "that deals more with the thrust and organization of rock," such as Weather Report and jazz-fusion drummers Alex Acuña, Bill Bruford (also sometimes a member of Yes, King Crimson, and other progressive rock bands), Peter Erskine, Omar Hakim, and Simon Phillips. He also revealed his appreciation for rock drummers such as Warren Cann (Ultravox), Phil Collins and Jerry Marotta (e.g., with Peter Gabriel), Stewart Copeland (the Police), Steve Jansen (the group Japan), Rod Morgenstein (Dixie Dregs), Andy Newmark, and Chris Sharrock (Icicle Works), and for reggae, juju (King Sunny Ade), and other world music (Fish 1986). Peart's childhood piano lessons probably explain his predilection for melodic percussion, from chimes and glockenspiels to marimbas, and, later, MIDI- and/or sample-based instruments, as well as his ongoing interest in jazz drumming. Many of the band's most diverse musical and stylistic influences appear on the band's next two albums: *Power Windows* (1985) and *Hold Your Fire* (1987).

Similarly reflecting Rush's diversity of influence, around 1982–1984 its opening acts included Golden Earring (Dutch, progressive-influenced pop-rock), John Butcher Axis (UK, experimental jazz), Marillion (UK, progressive rock), guitar-singer-songwriter Rory Gallagher (Irish, blues-influenced rock), Gary Moore (formerly of Irish band Thin Lizzy, hard rock), Nazareth (Scottish hard rock and heavy metal), and Red Rider (Canadian, hard pop-rock).

6

"AGAINST THE RUN OF THE MILL"

Rock/Technology Balance, 1985–1988

Long before the arrival of songwriter-producers in the 1980s, Rush produced or coproduced its studio albums for reasons of artistic integrity, not in order to assess their commercial potential. Moreover, to solidify its mostly non–Top 40 status, the band left decisions about the release of Rush singles almost entirely to its record companies. On the other hand, Rush was considered sufficiently mainstream in 1985 that Geddy Lee was one of the featured singers on the famine relief song "Tears Are Not Enough," by the Canadian "supergroup" Northern Lights. The band's next two albums in its continued "mainstream adjacency" were *Power Windows* (1985) and *Hold Your Fire* (1987).

POWER WINDOWS (1985)

For its 1985 and 1987 albums, Rush again recorded mainly in the UK (plus Montserrat and partly in Toronto), after five years recording at Le Studio near Morin Heights, Quebec. The band worked with UK coproducer Peter Collins, and it would work with him again for Rush's 1994 and 1996 albums. Lee explains: "The main reason we chose [Collins] is because he's a good song producer. He's not hung up on technical stuff—he focuses on the song" (Moleski 1985, 49). Collins's background included writing and producing jingles as well as producing techno-pop recordings. His production associates included programmer/keyboard-ist Andy Richards, who had recently worked with the UK dance-pop sensation Frankie Goes to Hollywood.

Hugh Syme's cover art for *Power Windows* shows a teenage boy holding a remote control at a window. Three weird-looking TV sets—presumably one for each member of Rush—stand askew behind him. The boy seems to want to explore the scary-looking world outside—probably meaning adulthood. The remote-controlled window, the TV sets, the lightning flash outside, and so on, provide visual puns for the album title. Lyrically, the album concerns various types of power and their sociological effects.

"The Big Money"

The opening song, "The Big Money," addresses the band's mixed feelings about media and industry contexts, and the band performs the song's music video mainly on a "Monopoly"-like set. The album cover's "remote boy" is occasionally featured, and the band members seem to get sucked into TV screens. Otherwise, however, the band somewhat downplays its use of technology. On Lee's part of the set, a stand holds several keyboards, but Lee plays a (normal-sized) Wal bass for most of the song. The tactic of playing a bass guitar contrasts with the much greater amount of technology (e.g., Lee's earlier compact/high-tech Steinberger bass) shown in certain videos for songs from 1984. During the song's main synthesizer segment, however, Lee simultaneously plays a keyboard and the Moog Taurus I pedals shown at the base of the keyboard stand. Peart's electronic drums and/or voice-derived samples are sometimes featured in the song. He triggers some of the samples with electronic drum pads, which blur his "electro-acoustic" contributions. Actual drums are used in the song's second introduction, and the video shows Peart playing them. That section, however, also includes keyboard parts and sample-based orchestral hits. This contrasts with Peart's frequent use of Simmons electronic drums in certain 1984 videos.

The chorus (in 4/4 time) uses a raw guitar sound from Lifeson, aggressive drumming from Peart (on a traditional, if large, rock kit), and active/"popping" bass guitar from Lee. Parts of the song's verses (which are in 6/4 time) include voice-like synthesizer sounds, vocal samples, and even samples of Lifeson's guitar. The first part of Lifeson's guitar solo features numerous keyboard, electronic, and sampled sounds, and some of the song's more elaborate keyboard parts probably feature Andy Richards—the studio associate and guest performer who played on parts of this album. Thus, much of the song explores mid-1980s extremes within traditional rock *and* electronic elements. It parallels the band's two-part ambivalence—about the music industry and about music technology. The verses of Peart's lyrics refer to mixed feelings or a love/hate relationship, such as "Sometimes pushing all the buttons; sometimes pulling out the plug," but the song also inscribes this idea musically. The song also exemplifies post-progressive rock: as with "New World Man," "Red Sector A," and "The Body Electric" (1982–1984) it avoids "odd meters" (e.g., 7/8) and includes only a very small amount of virtuosic melodic/rhythmic interplay.

"Grand Designs"

The chorus of the album's second song, "Grand Designs," refers to "life in two dimensions" as a "mass production scheme." It also suggests the band's continuing preference for going "against the run of the mill" and for "swimming against the stream." The first verse refers to "style without substance," thus implicating the numerous mid-1980s synth pop stylists who achieved considerable success without much of an ability to play instruments—"so much mind on the matter" that "the spirit gets forgotten about." The band transcends its use of music technology by bridging it with an ongoing "real instrument" acumen—to "break the surface tension with our wild kinetic dreams." The song's main synthesizer line uses a sample of an acoustic guitar transformed into a vaguely sitar-like sound. Chorus 2 features grand piano samples and synthesizer sounds programmed into a sequenced (otherwise virtually unplayable) montage of arpeggios. In other places, the band processes Neil Peart's voice through electronic effects, and he plays these on his Simmons electronic drums.

"Manhattan Project"

Rock musicians in the post-counterculture sometimes followed the earlier idea of producing technically compelling inventions first and asking questions later. Arguably, it is a male construction, and one person who did so was 1940s U.S. nuclear weapons coordinator J. Robert Oppenheimer. The album's third song, "Manhattan Project," concerns the drive toward technical prowess in the context of nuclear weaponry. In a related matter, hard-core Rush musician-fans (male and female) valued Lee, Lifeson, and Peart's technique, power, and so on.

Peart's lyrics are ambivalent about the inevitable "big bang" of nuclear weaponry. He wonders if it produced "more than [its inventors] bargained for." Along the same lines, Rush's tentative experiments with synthesizers in the 1970s swelled in the 1980s. The verses consistently include synthesized and sampled sounds, and the effect is one of technological irony. The song's chorus, however, features a more traditional Rush sound: a complex rhythm featuring guitar. A later instrumental section incorporates a string section and wordless vocals, in a vaguely Russian-sounding arrangement by Anne Dudley—of the UK techno band Art of Noise, a contributor to Frankie Goes to Hollywood, and later a successful, Oscar-winning film composer. The song ends cautiously, with a fade-out of Lifeson's main earlier guitar part and a return to Peart's "military" snare roll. The song succinctly combines aspects of progressive rock and post-punk/new-wave music.

"Marathon"

The fourth song, "Marathon," also uses a string section arrangement by Anne Dudley, as well as a wordless choral arrangement by UK musician-arranger Andrew Jackman. The song outlines Peart's desire not to burn out too fast. The song's verses mainly use traditional rock instruments (including Lee's active, "popping" bass), but its chorus focuses mainly on Lee's voice ("the peak is never passed," etc.) in combination with voice-like synthesizer chords and Peart's drumming. Lifeson's guitar features prominently in much of the instrumental 7/4 and 7/8 middle sections, but Lee features bass first and then keyboards to match Lifeson. Lee underscores the moralizing 7/4 bridge with keyboards: "You can do a lot in a lifetime, if you don't burn out too fast." The choral and orchestral contributions then join later versions of the song's chorus, which modulates optimistically upward by whole tone. (Christian rock musicians also frequently used this basic "transcendence" technique.) These elements, along with extensive overdubbing of Lee's voice, heighten the emotional effect of not burning out psychologically. The song concludes the first half of the album with a very long fade-out, suggesting that the song's optimism never really ends.

The Rest of *Power Windows*

The second half of *Power Windows* begins with "Territories," "Middletown Dreams," and "Emotion Detector." "Territories" concerns globalization versus regionalisms and includes a joke about everyone thinking they have "better beer." Peart avoids playing a snare drum in this song and instead features elaborate hi-hat rhythms, tom fills, and bongos. Peter Gabriel's world music influences in the early 1980s also often avoided snare drums. The vaguely pentatonic guitar and keyboard melodies also suggest world music influences. The chorus features held synthesizer chords and bass pedals, but other sections feature dance-like rhythmic guitar gestures. Peart puns on the word "indifferent" ("in different"), and Lee includes a sample of his voice on the words "round and round."

"Middletown Dreams" complements the suburban imagery of "Subdivisions" and "The Analog Kid" (both 1982) and the writer/dancer biographies of "Losing It" (also 1982) with lyrics about people whose dreams provide some "transport" concerning their lives: a salesman who relies on his hidden booze, a teenage guitarist who aspires to become "a brilliant shooting star," and a "middle-aged Madonna" with artistic ambitions. Peart selected "Middletown" as one of the most common "heartland" names for a small town teeming with such persons.

"Emotion Detector" begins with Lee playing a heavily layered synthesizer sound, to which the band gradually adds Peart's percussion sounds and Lifeson's guitar. Lifeson's guitar takes over toward the end, before a synth-heavy second introduction. Peart applies ambivalence to lyrics about relationships and feelings ("It's true that love can change us, but never quite enough"). Lee keeps his vocal range relatively low for much of the song, but for "throw ourselves wide open" (verse 1) he sings higher notes. Lee uses his PPG synthesizer for the song's higher melodies, and sequencers or arpeggiators also provide high keyboard parts in certain sections. Lifeson's guitar solo initially appears over a bass part by Lee that almost matches it in melodic importance. Later parts of the solo occur over a reprise of the song's relatively melodic, synthesizer-based second introduction. Peart sometimes plays his Simmons electronic drums in this song, but most often to trigger organic/ wooden-sounding samples. Toward the end of the song, the band pairs a recurring instrumental chordal "hook" with the words "feelings run high."

"Mystic Rhythms"

The album's eighth and final song, "Mystic Rhythms," also fits the album's themes of power and of the blurring of technology. As Geddy Lee explains:

> Everything in it is going through a synthesized something. We spent a day sampling African drums, tablas, roto-toms, and all kinds of bizarre sounds. We found four appropriate ones, locked into four different AMS's [delay units with sampling capabilities] that were triggered by Neil playing his Simmons kit. There's a very unique guitar sound, too. It's an Ovation acoustic guitar going through amplification and it comes off with a very synth-like sound. (Stern 1985)

The song's video also participates in these types of ambiguities: unlike the modern TV screens in the video for "The Big Money," the video for "Mystic Rhythms" incorporates old-fashioned variants of projection technology, thus somewhat recalling the trio of odd-looking TVs on the album cover. Images of water, reflection, and light (and nature generally) contrast with an elaborate mechanical toy, glowing spheres, a Claymation-like Godzilla, nautical-like portholes looking in on Rush, and a skeleton containing other beings. The skeleton and toy reflect the "embedded" nature of the song's sampled/synthesized soundscape, which comprises, for example, electronic drums consistently triggering sampled percussion, twice as much synthesizer "airtime" as bass guitar, and a few "seagull" noises reminiscent of the electronic bird sounds (a.k.a. the "music score") of Alfred Hitchcock's film *The Birds* (1963).

The melodies and chords of the song favor pentatonic elements (thus referencing "non-Western" constructions), and the lyrics refer to the natural/mystical world outside: "the unknown . . . a glimpse of what's beyond." Music technology can embed such "unknown" things, and, paralleling the song's opening buildup of materials, the song ends with an extended fade-out to a virtually inaudible—and thus technologically deceptive—synthesizer "real ending" to conclude the album. As Neil Peart puts it, the song provides a "good marriage of lyrics and music" (Pollock 1986). The NBC television network agreed, as it used "Mystic Rhythms" as the theme for its show 1986. Rush made one more album exploring the audible aspects of music technology (*Hold Your Fire*, 1987), before starting to move away from that in its subsequent new music.

HOLD YOUR FIRE (1987)

Rush's twelfth studio album, *Hold Your Fire*, includes the FM radio "album tracks" "Force Ten" and "Time Stand Still." The latter, including its video, features guest backup vocals by U.S. singer-songwriter Aimee Mann. She had recently been the lead singer of the band 'Til Tuesday, well known for its 1985 hit song "Voices Carry." On the album, Rush continued its use of synthesizers, samplers, and electronic percussion, and still often included eccentric instrumental middle sections in its songs. Peart also remained lyrically interested in such things as non-Western cultures and nature. In addition, the band again recorded the album mainly in the UK, with coproducer Peter Collins.

"Force Ten"

The album's opening song, "Force Ten," uses the maximum level of the Beaufort wind velocity scale as an analogy for the storms of life. Neil Peart based his lyrics on some ideas by Pye Dubois, who had earlier provided the genesis of Rush's best-known song ("Tom Sawyer," 1981). The band also wrote the song in just a few hours, thus paralleling the origin of Rush's only U.S. Top 40 song ("New World Man," 1982). The lyrics encourage the listener to transcend both the inability to predict things and the powerful forces that one cannot control. Peart was inspired by the writings of early twentieth-century U.S. writer Ernest Hemingway. Musically, a sampled choir, crowd sounds, and guitar begin the song, but these are followed by jackhammer samples and a woman's laugh—which are both meant to depict "powerful forces" comparable to the wind storm of the song's title.

Lee's main riff (open intervals, above a pedal tone) and Lifeson's related guitar derivations join Peart's powerful rock drumming. This music also underscores the song's vocal introduction: "Tough times demand tough talk, demand tough hearts, demand tough songs. . . ." The verses (in 4/4 time) use a call-and-response, back-and-forth pattern of Lee's vocals and Lifeson's guitar gestures. The lyrics similarly ebb and flow: "We can rise and fall like empires, flow in and out like the tide." The harmonies expand the open interval to additional notes. The song's bridge uses keyboards and fills in numerous chords and notes only implied earlier. This jarring move parallels the bridge's relatively positive lyrical take on things. A middle section returns to open intervals, but now in a different time signature: 6/4. Ethereal-sounding synthesizers accompany the song's mellow chorus: "Look in to the eye of the storm. Look out to the form without form." The instrumental section (in 4/4) initially features Lifeson's atmospheric guitar gestures. It then has a rhythmically eccentric section using "cross rhythms." The song ends with additional choruses (in 6/4 time) and then material that reprises the song's introduction (i.e., back in 4/4 time), including the earlier jackhammer sounds.

"Time Stand Still"

"Time Stand Still" (the album's second song) includes guest backup vocals by Aimee Mann. Her contributions provide an emotional resonance for some of the song's lyrics: "Time stand still: I'm not looking back, but I want to look around me now. Time stand still: see more of the people and the places that surround me now" and, especially, "Experience slips away. . . . The innocence slips away." The song has to do with the band's "progressive" desire to look outside of itself and to a wide variety of colleagues and influences. Mann also appears in the song's video as a movie camera operator and backup singer. The song's video uses "blue-screen" effects, in order to splice and move different elements around. The individual band members (with their instruments) and Mann (with the camera) thus often float around on a set or outside in nature. At the end of the song, the "innocence slips away," and Mann waves good-bye and magically disappears off into the background.

Peart used sampled Asian temple blocks at various pitches, and they are mainly combined with Lee's keyboards and Mann's guest vocals in the song's comparatively gentle chorus. The instrumental section (in 7/4 time) includes Lifeson's fairly elaborate guitar (though not really a "solo"), along with bass, drums, and some sampled sound effects. Lee's short, virtuosic bass flourishes appear in between various sections of the song.

The Rest of *Hold Your Fire*

Compared with "Force Ten" and "Time Stand Still," "Open Secrets" (the album's third song) contains a relatively large amount of synthesizer elements. Similarly, although their lyrics ostensibly address other things, the fourth and fifth songs, "Second Nature" and "Prime Mover," both self-consciously address Rush's use of music technology in this period and, revealingly (and like "Time Stand Still"), neither song includes a guitar solo. "Open Secrets" does have one, though, and Alex Lifeson discusses his approach:

> [Solos come from] the mood . . . created by the music. I suppose in a way that makes it attached to the lyrics. But it's more the music that provides the trigger for what the solo does. If it's a dark, melancholy sound to a particular song, then the solo will reflect that. An example is "Open Secrets." It has that lonely mood to it from a musical point of view. I think the solo in that song reflects that wailing loneliness. ("Interview with Alex Lifeson" 1988)

The video for the sixth song, "Lock and Key," features the colorful red balls (and, briefly, their juggler) that are also shown in Hugh Syme's album art. On the album cover, three balls—one each for Lee, Lifeson, and Peart—form a triangle. On the album's inner artwork, an old man juggles burning versions of these balls, also in a triangle.

Right from its opening gestures and throughout its first minute, "Lock and Key" relies heavily on synthesizers and samples, even though the video shows only a single keyboard. The song's video contrasts the colorful balls and studio set by inserting a number of brief, black-and-white classic movie "samples." These provide commentaries on certain lyrics: "terrible choice," "fanatical cause," and, especially, the title phrase "lock and key": a prisoner and his jail cell. Certain parts of the song extensively use overdubs of Geddy Lee's voice. Thus, the video *shows* Alex Lifeson singing, even though we *hear* two or more versions of Geddy Lee's voice. The video also inserts live concert footage for the (very brief) guitar solo and other instrumental sections. On the recording of this song, Lee plays a custom Wal bass with a fifth string tuned to a lower-than-usual note: somewhat below a bass guitar's normal lowest string. Although he could have achieved such low notes on a synthesizer, Lee wished to privilege his traditional instrument in a new, technological way.

The album's seventh song, "Mission," contains the line "Hold your fire"—the album title. The lyrics somewhat reprise the individualism that Peart earlier derived from Ayn Rand and Ernest Hemingway, and the title phrase refers not to its more obvious meaning of "Don't shoot," but to persevering with one's "burning desire" or "inner flame." The lyrics include a wide variety of relevant words: fire, burning, bright, flame, dream, ignite, spirit, vision, mission, passion, heart, power, instinct, drive, danger, imagination, focus, soar, ambition, desire, obsession, light, wish, spark, alive, action, pride, paradise. The song uses vaguely related major keys, recalling a similar construction in "Force Ten." The odd construction gives the song a suitably varied, yet positive-sounding, tonal underpinning for its wide array of positive lyrical terms. The middle instrumental section switches to 5/4 and a less-well-defined modal area ("flat 7"). Among the eccentric elements of this section, the band includes unusual, "augmented" chords, an elaborate rhythmic unison of Lee's bass with Peart's simultaneous layering of snare drum and marimba (played on a sampler via a KAT MIDI percussion controller), and Lifeson's strange, temporary move to "flat-side" harmonies. The lyrics immediately following the middle section state: "It's cold comfort to the ones without it." This means that successfully eccentric behavior, such as Rush's, can provide *real* comfort only to other people who establish realistic missions for themselves. Such an attitude could hardly be further from the counterculture.

"Turn the Page" (eighth) begins in a rhythmically fast 6/4 and shows signs of having originated in Geddy Lee's bass playing. The active bass part continues throughout the verses, but the vocal melody establishes quite different rhythmic syncopations and other patterns. Lee explains that it took him a long time to learn to play and sing this song simultaneously (Tolleson 1988). Harmonically, the song begins with certain features not unlike the tonally/modally inventive instrumental middle section of "Mission." The abrupt shifts parallel the lyrics about an extremely wide variety of elements encountered in a daily newspaper, and then the chorus (in 4/4) characterizes the newspaper (perhaps all media) as, at best, a time capsule or a wind tunnel: Is truth a moving target or is it just poorly lit? When we can't answer these things, "we disengage. We turn the page." Lifeson's blustery solo parallels the lyrics' "wind tunnel." "Tai Shan" (ninth) denotes Neil Peart's wonder at a holy mountain that he had visited in China. The flutelike sounds at the very beginning of the song evoke the Asian Shakuhachi flute. The band also includes samples of Asian percussion instruments (e.g., gongs and temple blocks).

The tenth and last song, "High Water," also inscribes a certain amount of exoticism, referring to endless floods, ocean spray, mountain springs, flowing marble fountains, mighty rivers, waves crashing on the shoreline, torrents of tropical rain, and the driving rain of redemption. The water "takes us home" and streams "down inside our veins," because our mammalian ancestors "broke the surface" and emerged from it. The song includes a substantial number of synthesizers and sampled sounds, including musical analogues for certain parts of the lyrics. Some of the keyboard parts use extensive flanging (or a similar digital technique), where the timbre changes slightly on each subsequent note or chord. The bass and drums seem comparatively basic, but Lifeson receives several brief guitar solo "windows." One section of the song includes a string arrangement composed and conducted by Steven Margoshes. Near the end, the song also includes backward samples of Aimee Mann's voice, for an eerie, exotic, but subtle, effect.

"I WANT TO LOOK AROUND ME NOW"

In its music and concert tours from 1980 to 1988, Rush expanded its ongoing strategy of "permanent change" by including influences from post-punk/new-wave rock, post-progressive hard rock, and jazz-rock fusion. Lyrically, the band addressed a wide spectrum of the human condition, including pride, freedom, fame, self-doubt, war, ambition, conflict, originality, burning out, vulnerability, outside forces, and loneliness. For Rush and its fans, its musical disposition involves the virtuosic interaction of guitar, bass, drums, and, to a lesser extent, voice. In the 1980s, Rush's manner of working allowed them to use music technology while still sounding like a version of the band that many people already knew. Instead of abandoning music technology as a problem around 1982, the band worked through certain tone color and textural possibilities and added these to its stylistic history. The band became especially enamored of sampling technology, and it sometimes sampled world music percussion instruments and other "natural" sounds (e.g., voices, machine noises, and even electric guitars) only to play them back in masked variants with keyboards, digital sequencers, and/or electronic drum triggers—thus subtly normalizing the process.

By 1987–1988, Lee's offstage equipment *also* included as many as four synthesizers (including two Roland modules), seven samplers (Akai 900 modules), and two Yamaha QX-1 sequencers. From 1984 to 1988, Rush also used the skills of engineers, mixers, synthesizer programmers, and/or sampler programmers such as Paul Northfield, Jim Burgess, and Andy Richards. Northfield contributed to a number of Rush and Rush-related projects from 1980 to 2002. Burgess ran the Toronto-based music technology consulting and retail firm Saved by Technology, and Rush credited that company (in the liner notes) with technical assistance until 1993. Session musician Andy Richards also contributed keyboard parts to certain Rush songs in 1985 and 1987. Despite all the technology, Lee suggests: "[Feel and melody] make a great, memorable song" and he valorizes "direct communication of expression" (Armbruster 1984, 61–62). The band's engagement with music technology in the mid- to late-1980s is especially evident in the recent songs performed on its third live album, *A Show of Hands* (1989, recorded in the UK and the US). The album includes Peart's elaborate drum solo, "The Rhythm Method."

From 1985 to 1988, Rush's opening acts included Marillion (UK, progressive rock); the Canadian bands FM (synthesizer-heavy progressive rock, reunited with eccentric/anonymous cofounder Nash the Slash) and Chalk Circle (indie rock); U.S. artists such as Blue Öyster Cult (hard rock), the Fabulous Thunderbirds (blues rock oriented), the Steve Morse Band (rock-jazz fusion), and Tommy Shaw (hard rock, formerly of Styx, soon to be of Damn Yankees and, later, of Styx again); and the European band the McAuley Schenker Group (a.k.a. MSG, hard rock, led by former Scorpions and UFO guitarist Michael Schenker). Only a few of these opening acts suggest the continuing progressive tendencies in some of Rush's music, although some of them fit with Rush's increased interest in music technology. Also, a number of Rush's opening acts suggest the band's interest in giving exposure to other Canadian bands. In any case, from 1989 to 2012 the band itself then gradually decreased the *sounds* of music technology while applying related *techniques* to its songwriting and arranging. That began with the album *Presto* (1989).

7

"IT'S HARD TO PLAY IT SAFE"

New Approaches to Being a Power Trio, 1989–1995

Starting on its three studio albums from 1989 to 1993, the band tapered off its interest in music technology in favor of somewhat reengaging the kinds of music it had inadvertently inspired: especially aspects of hard alternative rock and progressive heavy metal. "Show Don't Tell" (*Presto*, the band's debut on Atlantic Records, 1989), the Grammy-nominated instrumental "Where's My Thing?" (*Roll the Bones*, 1991), and "Stick It Out" (*Counterparts*, 1993) exemplify rhythmically complex, somewhat funk-inspired, yet relatively "hard"-sounding, songs. "The Pass" (*Presto*) reflects on teen angst and suicide and "Nobody's Hero" (*Counterparts*) similarly reflects on cultural "false heroes," while "Roll the Bones" (*Roll the Bones*, 1991) somewhat explores African-influenced lyrical themes and even a kind of "rap" music. In the 1990s, the band won three Juno Awards: Artist of the Decade for the 1980s and for *Presto* and *Roll the Bones*.

Rush provides an instructive example of the diffusion of postsynthesizer, microprocessor-based music technology after 1987–1988. From 1982 to 1987 the band organized much of its new music around a combination of traditional rock instruments (e.g., guitar, bass, drums) and electronically generated (i.e., synthesized, sampled) sounds. For live performances, the band continued to use related technology into the 1990s and 2000s. This included offstage samplers triggered from keyboards and pedals onstage. In its new music from 1989 to 2012,

Rush considerably diminished its use of audible electronics yet pervasively applied computer technology to its songwriting.

"BOYS' CAMP"

For each new studio album from 1980 to the 2000s, Rush's "phase 1" arranging/rehearsal period functioned something like summer camp—the band lived and worked together on "retreat" at a house outside of Toronto for a period of about a month or two. During these periods, the band members generally spent the weekends with their spouses and children. For example, with a daughter born in 1994, Lee drove home most nights in 1996. In the "camp" setting, Peart mainly worked on lyrics while Lee and Lifeson worked on music, but with quite a few discussions of a song's lyrics before Lee started devising suitable vocal melodies.

Around 1989–1991, Lee and Lifeson composed and arranged new songs by combining (1) cassette-based recordings (especially good for capturing "jamming") with (2) eight-track, reel-to-reel recording/mixing, and (3) computer-based music sequencing (MIDI) software. Relevant software included Mark of the Unicorn's Performer on Macintoshes. Eventually one track of each completed eight-track song demo triggered—using SMPTE time code—the necessary synthesizer, sampler, and drum machine elements in sync with the guitar, bass, and vocal recordings on the seven other tracks (see Widders-Ellis 1991). From 1993 to 2001, Lee and Lifeson often used a fully digital, computer-based approach to combine all electronic and "acoustic" elements of a song demo in a single place: a computer's hard disk. In 1993, they used Steinberg's Cubase Audio, and in 1996 they used Emagic's Logic Audio. By 1996, Lee and Lifeson did their songwriting jamming onto Pro Tools professional hard disk recording software. All three programs ran on Macintosh computers.

From stereo mixes of completed song demos (e.g., mixed onto standard cassettes or, in the 1990s, onto digital audio tapes—DATs—or entirely on computer), the three band members further rehearsed the songs. For example, Peart prepared real drum parts (especially vis-à-vis a song's pacing, dynamics, and other "support requirements") and Lifeson worked out his guitar solos. Later, at a fully professional recording studio ("Stage 2"), the band transferred its demos (eight-track reel-to-reel or multitrack computer files) onto twenty-four-track equipment. At that point, the band and its coproducer and engineer spent about eight to ten additional weeks further refining the material and professionally recording the eventual album in at least one full-scale studio.

Despite getting "carried away" with computers, only a few of Rush's fifty-six new songs released between late 1989 and early 2002 use the audible side of music technology in more than a secondary capacity. Many instances of synthesizers and/or samplers prove nearly unnoticeable except when loudly amplifying certain songs. Nearly every review of a new Rush studio album from 1989 to 2002 focused on the band's abandoning of keyboards since the last album. In reality, *Presto* (1989) accomplished the most significant change along these lines, and the subsequent four studio albums reinforced it. In a parallel move, only a few Rush songs from 1989–2002 make use of 1970s/early-1980s, progressive-style asymmetrical time signatures. Instead, the band often uses more "organic"-sounding cross rhythms, occasional dropped beats (e.g., occasional bars of 2/4 while otherwise in 4/4), or contrasting sections in alternate time signatures, such as 6/4 or 3/4 when otherwise in 4/4.

Rush's new songs from 1989 to 2002 reduced the sounds of 1970s/early-1980s progressive rock and of mid-1980s music technology to occasional or residual status. Concurrently, the band's traditional guitar/bass/drums approach reemerged. Though less noticeable audibly as "progress," hard disk recording and arranging dominated the band's practice—its compositional application of music technology.

PRESTO (1989)

On *Presto* (1989), only "Red Tide" (track 9), "Available Light" (track 11), and, to a somewhat lesser extent, "War Paint" (track 4) and "Anagram (for Mongo)" (track 8), feature synthesizers or samplers more than incidentally or subtly. Even the sequencing of these four tracks suggests a significant downplaying of audible music technology on the first two-thirds of the album. The band's four studio albums from 1982 to 1987 differ significantly from this. The fact that coproducer Rupert Hine, who had previously worked with the Fixx, Tina Turner, and others, similarly resisted the use of digital technology suggests that Lee had already largely abandoned keyboards in the pre-Hine songwriting period at "Boys' Camp." After recording mostly in the UK circa 1985–1987, Rush returned to recording mostly in Canada, at Quebec's Le Studio (1989–1993) and at Toronto's McClear (1989–1996) and Reaction Studios (1996–2001).

The magic/nature aspect of *Presto* appears in Hugh Syme's grayscale cover art of eleven rabbits sitting on a small hill. Most of these animals appear in the lower foreground, taking up nearly half of the cover. An inverted magician's top hat hovers over the hill's peak in the middle background, with a twelfth rabbit peaking over the hat's rim. The images suggest that the first eleven rabbits emanated from the hat's "magic." This presumably represents Rush's posttechnology stylistic direction, as in "Presto Change-O." (Also, "presto" means "quickly" in Italian.) The eleven rabbits on the ground may thus represent the album's eleven songs, with the twelfth rabbit suggesting "more to come" from the band on its new record label and/or with less use of music technology. The ominous clouds behind the hill (and on the back cover) similarly suggest a magical "change in the weather." As if not to take this too seriously, each concert during Rush's later *Counterparts* tour (1993–1994) included the ritual shooting down of balloon effigies of these same rabbits, as if to say: "We're still changing."

Presto's CD booklet includes, in addition to the lyrics, Andrew MacNaughtan's portrait of each band member as well as Syme's graphic indicating the game rock-paper-scissors. This relates to the album's second-last song, "Hand over Fist." Rock-paper-scissors also appears as one of Syme's numerous groupings for the ornate folded inlay for Rush's later album, *Counterparts* (1993).

"Show Don't Tell"

On *Presto* (1989), Rush's funk/groove-inspired playing infuses the band's music at least as much as music technology. Keyboards, although still present for about half of "Show Don't Tell," provide only a small amount of timbral color compared to the guitar, bass, and drums. Lee plays bass for most of the song and lets sequencers (or coproducer Rupert Hine or keyboard associate Jason Sniderman) play most of the keyboard parts. Moreover, Lee plays a quite elaborate bass solo during the song's middle section, and the band also gives a large portion of the song to "neo-progressive" virtuosic unison passages. Lifeson, although his guitar participates through most of the song, does not play more than a few seconds of solo-like material, and the song also includes no asymmetrical time signatures. However, the highly complex main unison riff more than makes up for such a lack of traditional "progressive" elements and provides a good example of the band's direction away from mathematical/metrical playing (and away from music technology) and toward a more emotional and rhythmic style of playing. Indeed, the song reached No. 1 on *Billboard*'s chart of Rock Album Tracks.

Funk-like aspects include the extended chord tones, the pause after the opening sixteenth-note flourish, the rhythmic anticipation into the second beat of the second measure, the chromatic melody inflections, the inconsistencies between the guitar and bass notes at the beginning of the fourth bar, and certain metrical compressions. As Peart says of this song's music:

> "Show Don't Tell" begins with a syncopated guitar riff that appears two or three times throughout the song. That was about the hardest thing for me to find the right pattern for. I wanted to maintain a groove and yet follow the bizarre syncopations that the guitar riff was leading into. It was demanding technically, but at the same time, because of that, we were determined that it should have a rhythmic groove under it. It's not enough for us to produce a part that's technically demanding; it has to have an overwhelming significance musically. So it had to groove into the rest of the song and it had to have a pulse to it that was apart from what we were playing. (Miller 1989)

Of its lyrics, he said: "I adopted an attitude and character. I took a stance and a good attitude and developed it. . . . I find a trend for us since *Grace under Pressure* [1984] has been cutting off abstractions" (Krewen 1990). The "adopted attitude" seems to suggest that apart from our closest friends, people should not expect us to believe what they say. Peart couches the lyrics in courtroom imagery: due reflection, objections, judge, jury, evidence, order in the court, witness take the stand, exhibit A, and so on. Given that he calls this a "good attitude" and given his mixed feelings about fame in "Limelight" (*Moving Pictures*, 1981), one might infer at least a partially autobiographical slant to these lyrics. As for the musical direction of *Presto*, the songs "Scars," "Superconductor," and "Hand over Fist" also include certain groove elements related more to funk than to progressive rock or hard rock.

The Rest of *Presto*

"Chain Lightning," the album's second song, applies Peart's interest in nature and meteorological events (e.g., "sun dogs" and meteor showers) to the idea of human response and shared experiences. He also somewhat relates these ideas to his recent travel experiences and to his family. This interest in nature, also apparent in two of the album's later songs ("Red Tide" and "Available Light"), relates somewhat to Peart's lyrics for "Jacob's Ladder" and "Natural Science" (both on *Permanent Waves*, 1980) but now applied less abstractly. Peart also wrote nature-referencing song lyrics in the mid-1980s: "Distant Early Warning" (the opening song of *Grace under Pressure*, 1984), "Force Ten," "Tai Shan," and "High Water" (the first and last two songs of *Hold Your Fire*, 1987). The music includes frantic-sounding accounts of nature and people (e.g., energy, laughter, hope, dreams), rhythmically emphatic responses to these things (e.g., respond, vibrate, feedback, resonate), and a comparatively relaxed chorus (e.g., "When the moment dies, the spark still flies, reflected in another pair of eyes").

In the album's third song, "The Pass," Peart demythologizes teen suicide, thus somewhat recalling his demythologizing of fame in "Limelight" (*Moving Pictures*, 1981) and of nuclear weapons in "Manhattan Project" (*Power Windows*, 1985). The song also previews his demythologizing of the empty term "hero" in "Nobody's Hero" (*Counterparts*, 1993). Its music grows emotionally from texturally stripped-down and rhythmically methodical verses into more heavily orchestrated choruses, including background vocals and some keyboards. The lyrics address the young person in the second person, presumably from the perspective of a concerned parent trying to get somewhat inside the kid's head. The chorus (including the ending of the song) inscribes a texturally and emotionally rich tone: "Turn around and walk the razor's edge; don't turn your back and slam the door on me," but the last half of this always thins to just Lee's lead vocal.

The song's video, revived on film during Rush's concert tours from 2002 to 2013, shows a teenage "burnout" (a white male, with long hair) glumly wandering around his school and then literally teetering on the edge of falling to his death. However, he doesn't go through with it. This ultimately provides the positive suggestion that many young people feel this way but that very few take this final step. The boy's smirk at the end of the video seems to suggest: "You don't think I'm *that* stupid, do you?" The parental perspective in the lyrics of "The Pass" encourages the kind of responsibility (e.g., meaningful conversations with one's children) sardonically shown to be lacking on the late-1990s/2000s TV show (and 1999 movie) *South Park.*

Although the following song, "War Paint" (fourth) also addresses suburban teen contexts, other songs on the album address a wide variety of topics. "War Paint" comprises two parallel stories, the first about a pregnant teen who disguises herself in order to escape her present circumstances and the second about a boy (probably the girl's boyfriend) who simultaneously disguises himself in order to "take the princess." Both mistake their "dreams for self-delusion."

"Scars" (fifth) includes a pervasive use of sampled Western and non-Western percussion instruments, which Peart played live via a KAT MIDI controller. This recalls his multisample pattern for "Mystic Rhythms" (*Power Windows*, 1985). Peart's lyrics use the imagery of scars (of pleasure and of pain) to refer, among other things, to positive and negative psychological imprints. Although he resisted deeming the song autobiographical, some of the images clearly resulted from his recent extended trips to China and Africa: a mountaintop (see "Tai Shan," *Hold Your Fire*, 1987), Serengeti nights, hungry child, desert, and clouds of flies.

The album's title song, "Presto" (sixth), includes magic/disguise imagery and the phrase "If I could wave my magic wand," but it otherwise suggests a preference for dreams and "second sight" over an overt belief in magic. "Superconductor" (seventh) applies the title term from physics and electrical engineering to the wildly popular (i.e., resistance-free) illusions created by pop stars. Ironically, the song's funkiest parts inscribe the album's only instance of an asymmetrical time signature: 7/4. Probably to parallel the lyrics about the artificiality (orchestrated "magic") of pop stars, the 4/4 sections sound more like "power pop," and one critic responded to Lifeson's use of powerful guitar figures—even in more "pop-oriented" songs—as "cathedral strength fretwork."

"Anagram (for Mongo)" (eighth) builds largely on "words games" (rarely actual anagrams), where one or more words in a line of the lyrics derive from the available letters in another, usually larger, word in the same phrase. Peart named the song after a character in *Blazing Saddles* (Mel Brooks's 1974 film comedy) who receives a bomb disguised as a "Candygram for Mongo!" (Neil Peart, *Rush Backstage Club* newsletter, October 1991). This gives a good sense of Rush's subtle sense of humor. The song's verses musically recall late-1970s "arena rock."

Ironically, *Presto*'s two most synthesizer-oriented songs, "Red Tide" and "Available Light" (ninth and eleventh), both concern physical nature rather than human nature. The former refers to the "new plagues" of acid rain, ozone holes, and industrial waste. Lee's syncopated, brass-like synthesizer patterns never quite fit the diatonic, straight-eighths (presumably sequenced) piano pattern. This parallels the fact that these elements contradict the comparative anti-music-technology tone of the album's first eight songs. Here, the use of music technology parallels Peart's concerns about the effects of other kinds of technology on the environment. Peart borrowed the term "red tide" from oceanic micro-biology, and some of his lyrics paraphrase "Do Not Go Gently into That Good Night" by the Welsh poet Dylan Thomas. Lifeson also parallels Peart's environmental concerns in his sputtering, angry guitar solo. The guitar solo briefly replaces Lee's syncopated brass patterns over the piano sequence.

The album's closing (eleventh) song, "Available Light," refers to a restless wind, full moon, sea and sky, city canyons, crying buildings, echoes, the four winds, tricks of light, shadows, and so on. One line suggests a reference to the title of Rush's 1981 album *Moving Pictures*: "Trick of light, moving picture, moments caught in flight make the shadows darker or the colours shine too bright." In its verses, the song initially uses piano chords as the main accompanying instrument to Lee's voice. (In this case, a sequencer or MIDI pedals provide the bass part for much of the song.) In the second verse, which the rock-style chorus nudges up a tone, Lifeson heightens the gentle "soft jazz" piano/voice/drum texture with blues-like, call-and-response phrases that interact with Lee's vocals. Shortly after *Presto*, Rush released a two-CD anthology (and related video collection), *Chronicles* (1990). It mostly comprises a chronological survey of selected songs from the band's Mercury Records era, plus "Show Don't Tell."

ROLL THE BONES (1991)

On *Roll the Bones*, only the title track (with its brass stabs, organ glissandos, and occasional subtle pads), the Grammy-nominated instrumental "Where's My Thing?" and, to a lesser extent, "Dreamline" and "Neurotica" use synthesizers or samplers more than incidentally. The sequence of these four comparatively technological songs (tracks 3, 5, 1, and 9 of 10) seems less "end weighted" than the four on Rush's previous album (tracks 4, 8, 9, and 11 of 11). *Roll the Bones* contains no particularly fast songs, which thus often facilitates flow/groove elements. Also, almost every song falls into the key of E and/or A, which allows for Lee's relatively low bass guitar parts and similarly low (i.e., midnatural range) vocals and also frees up overtone frequency space for Lifeson's guitars.

Neither the members of Rush nor the band's fans ever abandoned their confidence in Rush's capabilities as rock instrumentalists. Thus, 1991 became something of a banner year for the members of Rush as performers. They achieved several reader-based "life's work" distinctions in musician-oriented magazines. This began in 1983–1986 with Peart in *Modern Drummer*, but it otherwise peaked in 1991. The readers of *Bass Player* voted Geddy Lee its Best Rock Bassist at least six times (including 1993), and it inducted him into its Hall of Fame. In 1991 the readers of *Guitar Player* voted Lee its first Bassist of the Year, and it later inducted him into its Bass Hall of Fame. In 1991 *Guitar for the Practicing Musician* recognized Alex Lifeson's similar accomplishments (1983–1991) and inducted him into its Hall of Fame. He achieved similar distinctions in *Guitar Player* and *Guitar World*.

"Dreamline"

The album's opening song, "Dreamline," grew from a short story co-written by Neil Peart and science-fiction writer (and Rush fan) Kevin J. Anderson. "Dreamline" repeated the distinction of the opening track of 1989's *Presto* ("Show Don't Tell") by reaching No. 1 on *Billboard*'s chart of Rock Album Tracks. The song appeared as the opening track on K-Tel/Warner's *Today's Hottest Hard Rock*. The lyrics refer to several restless characters traveling along highways and through deserts, and the first verse also suggests a possible science-fiction context ("a roadmap of Jupiter," "straight to the heart of the sun"), but the second verse refers to Las Vegas and to "a star map of Hollywood." The band bases the song's verses around Lifeson's picked-electric-guitar arpeggios (even 4/4 eighth notes, centered on a minor key) and the choruses around a much louder, hard rock sound. A brassy synthesizer part also appears in the chorus, but it follows the chords and rhythms already present in the guitar, bass, and drums, and some of the sampled material provides the sound of passing cars. The song contains no "odd meters," the "groove" aspects also compensate for the lack of complicated/ "progressive" metrical constructions, and the song also features a fairly high degree of background vocals.

"Bravado"

"Bravado," the album's second song, suggests an extension of Peart's interest in individualism in the direction of social responsibility, as in "We will pay the price, but we will not count the cost." Speaking of Peart's masterly drumming, Lee describes the end of this song as "an example of limb independence that rivals any drummer, anywhere" (*Roll the Bones* radio premiere broadcast, 1991). For his part, Peart enthused about the bandmates' ability to come up with interesting rhythmic things using MIDI and drum machines. Generally, Lee and Lifeson prepare songs quite fully during the writing/arranging stage and then leave it to Peart to arrange and rehearse his drum and percussion parts. However, for Lifeson's guitar solos on "Bravado" (second) and "Ghost of a Chance" (eighth), Peart had already worked out his musical contributions to what the guitarist meant to be temporary, "throwaway" solos.

"Roll the Bones" (The Song)

The album's title song, "Roll the Bones" (third), borrows African diasporic language for fate or change, and it also relates to the dice imagery used in the song. As Peart's lyrics put it: "We draw our own designs, but fortune has to make that frame" and "Fate is just the weight of circumstances." This updates Peart's lyrics for "Freewill" (*Permanent Waves*, 1980) from vaguely Randian atheistic individualism to vaguely left-wing agnostic libertarianism. The line also suggests a reference to

Rush's "Circumstances" (*Hemispheres*, 1978). Loud, brass-like synthesizer stabs occasionally reinforce the verses' ambiguous spin on fate, and a similarly loud "organ" glissando introduces the somewhat funkier bridge. The chorus then features some overdubbed vocals, comparatively subtle organ-like keyboard chords, and Lifeson's strummed acoustic guitar, which is present during nearly half of the song.

Lifeson's electric-guitar solo (accompanied by acoustic guitar) follows the second chorus, but as he "trails off," a drastic textural change occurs: electronic percussion replaces Peart's otherwise traditional drumming and a thumpy, synthesized bass line replaces Lee's bass playing. More strikingly, though, a digitally modified—and quite low—version of Lee's spoken voice presents Peart's eccentric approximation of rapping (at 3:11–3:41 and 3:51–4:12). The song's MTV-style video (and concert footage) features a skeleton head performing the "rap." Lifeson's preceding guitar solo segues into the rap section, he continues to provide blues-derived "squeals" into the new section, and an instrumental version of the song's hard rock chorus appears halfway through. All of this suggests that the band felt some ideological discomfort in referencing rap music in this way.

The band gave the rap a rather weird vocal sound, delayed the section's entrance until well into the song (3:11–4:12 of 5:30), inserted an instrumental reference to the song's much more rock-oriented chorus in between the rap's two phrases, and ended the song with repetitions of the song's hard rock chorus (eventually faded). This recalls the pseudo-reggae insertions and subsequent hard rock of the end of Rush's "The Spirit of Radio" (*Permanent Waves*, 1980). However, unlike the reggae/ska rhythmic elements circa 1981–1984, the band did not pursue rap elements after 1991.

The Rest of *Roll the Bones*

The album's fourth song, "Face Up," begins with electric-guitar arpeggios, active drumming, and minimal bass guitar. Repetitions of the same pattern add keyboards and Lee's active bass. Similar music underlies the verses; then the chorus abandons the keyboards for a more hard rock sound. The bridge softens the texture considerably for introspective lyrics about the negatives and positives of being alone. The following brief, "freewheeling" guitar solo suggests approval at the positive "spin" (literally) taken at the end of the bridge. Lifeson's solo briefly approximates the revving of a car engine, although Peart may have had in mind bicycling. Lifeson's engine revving slightly resembles aspects of Rush's well-known car song, "Red Barchetta" (*Moving Pictures*, 1981).

Although the band had attempted to write an instrumental piece for *Presto* (1989), it kept using the resultant music in other songs. Finally, in 1991 "Where's My Thing?" (placed fifth and humorously subtitled "Part IV, 'Gangster of Boats' Trilogy") successfully followed Rush's previous Grammy-nominated instrumental, "YYZ" (*Moving Pictures*, 1981). Similarly to "YYZ" losing in 1981 to the Police's "Behind My Camel," "Where's My Thing?" lost in 1992 to guitarist Eric Johnson's "Cliffs of Dover." Significantly, Rush thought highly of the Police in the late 1970s and early 1980s, and Alex Lifeson thought highly of Eric Johnson in the late 1980s and early 1990s. Johnson opened some Rush shows in the early 1990s.

The instrumental's opening section features Lifeson's riff combining fast-strummed sixteenth notes and syncopated chord hits. The texturally homophonic second section includes loud, synthesized filter sweeps at the beginning of its phrases and a kind of call-and-response between the keyboard and guitar. The texturally busier third section varies considerably in dynamics, adds a few extra beats from time to time, and also includes a brief guitar solo. The form is fairly complex among its three main sections, and it derives from the possibilities inherent in Lee and Lifeson's computer-based, multisectional song-arranging techniques.

The song after the instrumental, "The Big Wheel" (sixth), refers semiautobiographically to a kid who does a "slow fade" from a "ready-made faith" and chases "something new to believe in." Peart appreciated some of the symbolism and language of religion, but denied any specific autobiographical intent in this song. The title of the following (seventh) song, "Heresy," suggests that it might pick up on some of the themes of "The Big Wheel." Instead, it reflects ideologically on the "wasted years" of the Cold War ("Bombs and basement fallout shelters, all our lives at stake") and the establishment of capitalism in the former Soviet Union and the former East Germany ("The counter-revolution at the counter of a store: people buy the things they want and borrow for a little more").

"Heresy" begins with faded-in military drums, but its musical temperament otherwise uses a softer rock style to suggest accommodation ("forgiving at last," "saying goodbye to the past"). Lifeson used detuned folk-rock, acoustic-guitar sounds to parallel the song's unusual political lyrics, and Peart incorporated a rhythmic element inspired by his travels in Africa. This recalls the integration of world music elements into Western popular music in the 1980s and early 1990s by Peter Gabriel, Paul Simon, David Byrne, and others. Although Peart traveled in Africa and China mainly for reasons other than to experience non-Western music, he sometimes performed informally with master drummers and other musicians. Related "world" ideas appear in Hugh Syme's album cover, including a wall of dice of which the backdrop of the upper portion shows the number three on each surface. The rest of the wall spells out the band name and the album name in contrasting colors and numbers. In front, a boy has just kicked the head of a skeleton along a sidewalk. The back cover includes three bones, presumably part of the same skeleton, flying through a window in a segment of the dice wall from the front cover. Peart suggests that the album art references European symbols and techniques, such as the seventeenth-century Dutch style called "vanitas" (Peart 1993).

The album's eighth song, "Ghost of a Chance," functions as a kind of love song, an area that Peart addresses in only a few Rush songs. Lee and Lifeson referred to the "twangy—almost rockabilly" guitar riff at the beginning of this song as the "spy part." For the verses of "Neurotica" (ninth) Lee plays string-like synthesizer chords and bass pedals. Lee's real bass doubles the guitar riff in the bridge, but the keyboards also continue. The harmonic motion increases again for the keyboard-laden chorus, and a contrasting, wordless vocalization ("Oh . . .") falls consistently in between Lee's main phrases of the lyrics. The semi-psychological lyrics address someone else's insecurity, loss of nerve, hiding in their shell, and so on. The chorus uses a sequence of rhyming words, some real and some related to real words: neurotica, exotica, erotica, hypnotica, psychotica, chaotica. This recalls "Anagram (for Mongo)" on the previous album (*Presto*, 1989), but it also relates to two additional new songs.

For the final (tenth) song, "You Bet Your Life," the band attempted to emulate the kind of ebb-and-flow energy that effectively energized certain mainstream hard rock songs of the late 1980s and early 1990s.

Lifeson and the album's engineer used delay effects to get the kind of "see-sawing" quality also noticeable in music by U2. The song also includes a section of rhythmically "chanted," mantra-like recitation of numerous sociocultural contradictions. The band probably included such elements to mitigate the more extensive rap-like section in the album's title song, "Roll the Bones."

COUNTERPARTS (1993)

Counterparts (1993) reunited Rush with its 1985–1987 coproducer Peter Collins, but now, as with the two preceding studio albums coproduced with Rupert Hine, recorded in Canada. Only the occasional organ- or string-like elements of "Animate" (the opening song), the synthesizer chords and organ and bell sounds in the instrumental "Leave That Thing Alone" (ninth of eleven), and the piano near the end of "Cut to the Chase" (third) use synthesizer- or sampler-related elements more than incidentally. The band selected Kevin "Caveman" Shirley, a South African hard rock mixer, engineer, and producer (Aerosmith, the Black Crowes, etc.), to record *Counterparts*.

Once again, the album art also reflects the album's theme. Hugh Syme's front cover displays the rather obvious counterpart of a diagrammed nut and bolt. This sparseness reflects the album's comparatively hard-sounding style, but it also indicates the male-female counterparts examined on parts of the album. Syme's back cover shows a broken triangle with a Pac-Man-like shape (a circle with a "mouth" cut out) facing each side. The three faces thus complete the broken triangle, referring simultaneously to the band and to the album title. *Counterparts'* elaborate inner artwork features well over one hundred additional visual and textual counterparts (i.e., pairs and trios). These include the symbols for yin and yang, male and female, Adam and Eve, King and Queen face cards, sun and moon, and heads and tails (of a Canadian quarter). They also include rock-paper-scissors (reprising inner album artwork from *Presto*, 1989), a mortar and pestle, a musical note and a rest, a bow and arrow, a tortoise and a hare (and other animal pairs), see-hear-say no evil, a home and visitor sign (one of several indications of Geddy Lee's fascination with baseball), happy and sad pantomime masks, money and heart, and the Three Stooges (a frequent, self-effacing Rush symbol). The artwork also includes visual puns on a drum set, a sink fixture ("counter parts"), and the inner workings of a watch.

"Animate"

According to Peart, for the album's opening song, "Animate," he "used a basic R&B rhythm that I played back in my early days, coupled with that hypnotic effect that a lot of the British bands of the turn of the '90s had—bands like Curve and Lush" (Miller 1994). The band also ended up naming the album after the song's idea of counterparts. In a related move toward "tastefulness" and "conciseness," Geddy Lee discussed his greatly increased participation on lead and background vocals in the late 1980s and early 1990s, especially writing strong vocal melodies as a part of the early songwriting process and adding a lot more vocal harmonies.

"Stick It Out"

The album's second song, "Stick It Out," most prominently demonstrates the album's tendency toward stylistic/overdriven hardness and textural sparseness. In the verses, Lee and Lifeson's distorted riff alternates with Lee's vocal phrases. The title/chorus phrase suggests a play on words of encouraging the arrogant display of sticking out one's tongue (or perhaps one's middle finger) and encouraging endurance—to "stick it out." The verses rhythmically feature sparse but highly complex cross rhythms, especially between the main riff and the rest of the music. The song contains only a small number of subtle keyboards, and the frequent backing vocals provide a more visceral emotional resonance.

In an aural pun, Lifeson accompanies the words "safely restrained" and "carefully trained" with controlled feedback on his overdriven, sustained notes. The vocal triplets on "trust to your (instinct)" and "safely re(strained)" provide a similar "calming" effect. Moreover, much of the song features a careful controlling of the main riff's tritone (augmented fourth). For example, a compressed (one-bar) version of the riff also underlies the chorus, but it moves everything ahead by a quarter note and decorates one particular pitch in a fast, trill-like figure.

Regarding one of the verses, Peart refers to Latin influences and to a "Weather Report–type [jazz-rock fusion] effect." He also refers to the "tricky turn-arounds in the ride cymbal pattern, where it goes from downbeat to upbeat accents—anything I could think of to make it my own" (Miller 1994). His last five words—"to make it my own"—indicate something of Peart's conception of staying musically current and yet sticking it out as something that still sounds like Rush. Peart once referred to Rush as a "big musical sponge," meaning that the band "react[ed] to the times in a genuinely interested fashion" (electronic dance music, world beat, ska, etc.) rather than merely jumping on bandwagons. Peart means that the band "translates" other music back into its own (Dome 1988).

"Cut to the Chase"

As with the solos for "Bravado" and "Ghost of a Chance" (both on *Roll the Bones*, 1991), on "Cut to the Chase" (the album's third song) Lifeson's colleagues convinced him to retain his song demo "throwaway solos." Peart's lyrics apply various images of energy and potential from science, sport, and nature (e.g., combustion, archery, and desire) to the idea of an individual's possibilities for change and development. The *middle* section seemingly comes to terms with middle *age*, such as "I'm young enough to remember the future and the way things ought to be." (Peart turned forty in September of 1992, and his colleagues turned forty in the late summer of 1993, just before the album's release in October.) A transition just after this middle section self-consciously bounces the word "cut" back and forth between the left and right speakers. This technological effect and the related compression effect on that word slightly suggest the emerging use of such techniques in DJ, remix, and trip-hop music of the 1990s. Thus, it also suggests a nod toward "staying current."

"Nobody's Hero"

The album's fourth song, "Nobody's Hero," takes a difficult, and arguably politically incorrect, view of heroes. Peart's lyrics suggest that we should not, for example, *necessarily* interpret as a hero a gay man who dies of AIDS (verse 1) or a brutalized young woman (the verse 2 vignette suggests she was raped and/or murdered). They also suggest that in such matters we should certainly let a "shadow cross our hearts" and "try to hold some faith in the goodness of humanity." Peart carefully explained in interviews that these two main vignettes involved real people he knew or knew about:

> The first verse [is] about the first gay person that I knew and what a great example he set for me for what a gay person is, and prevented me from ever becoming homophobic. And [concerning] the second verse I happened to know this family that this terrible tragedy had happened to, and I thought of what a hole in their lives the girl had left behind. These were people who had more impact around than any hero, but at the same time in our Western way, they were nobody's hero. (Gehret 1994)

However, he never quite clarifies whether or not they should be held up as heroes.

At the end of the two folklike verses, featuring Lifeson's strummed acoustic guitar and Lee's "authentic" baritone chest voice (i.e., exclusively featuring them in verse 1), the line "But he's [or she's] nobody's hero" elides from the word "hero" into the musically more emphatic choruses. The choruses switch to rock-style, including electric guitar, bass, drums, and higher vocals, but they still mostly retain the acoustic guitar as well. They begin with brief descriptions of unambiguous heroes (or role models), such as someone who saves a drowning child, cures a wasting disease, lands a crippled airplane, solves great mysteries, voices reason against the howling mob, or even just does one's best job in his or her situation.

The song's choruses end with examples of unambiguous *anti*heroes (i.e., conventional heroes), including a handsome actor (who sometimes plays the *role* of a hero), soul-selling glamour stars (female *and* male), and a champion athlete (even when he or she plays a perfect game). Significantly, these sections musically combine Lifeson's acoustic and electric guitars throughout. Moreover, to further amplify the textural/textual split between the two types of heroes, the choruses more prominently feature a string arrangement. (It probably replaced a sampled or synthesized string part in the original "Boys' Camp" versions of the song, and in a few sections subtle keyboards may, in fact, be present.) After the first chorus, Lifeson's first electric-guitar solo, also subtly accompanied by the song's nearly pervasive acoustic guitar, facilitates the transition to the acoustically accompanied verse 2. After a second, longer electric guitar solo, the chorus—including the textural/textual split (and strings)—features heavily at the end of the song (including the fade-out).

The song uses prominent acoustic guitars as well as a string section, arranged and conducted by Michael Kamen (1948–2003). Among other things, Kamen founded and participated in the late-1960s/early-1970s rock/classical-oriented New York Rock & Roll Ensemble, worked with David Bowie in the 1970s, and later composed a number of film scores and film songs. He also arranged and conducted Metallica's performances with the San Francisco Symphony (released as *S&M* [*Symphony & Metallica*], 1999) and worked with Coldplay and members of the New York Philharmonic during the 2003 Grammy Awards ceremony.

"Nobody's Hero" provides the main exception to the album's rule of mainly featuring prominent electric guitar, bass, and drums. Rush stayed current largely by updating its pre-music-technology roots as a power trio. Thus, many songs on *Counterparts* sound something like certain elements of early 1990s hard alternative rock (e.g., Nirvana, Pearl Jam, and Soundgarden) or the progressive-oriented side of late-1980s and early-1990s hard rock and heavy metal (e.g., Dream Theater, Metallica, Pantera, and Queensrÿche). Many such artists cited Rush as an influence, so the band may have wished to reciprocate. In any case, the band certainly became much more interested in funk/groove influences than would have seemed likely given its emphasis on progressive, technical "math" rhythms in the late 1970s and early 1980s. Around the same time, Lee mentioned his interest in younger rock bands with actively rhythmic bass playing, such as Primus (which opened for Rush in 1992 and 1994) and the Red Hot Chili Peppers, both of which had grown up listening to Rush's music.

The Rest of *Counterparts*, Including "Relationship Songs"

For "Between Sun & Moon" (the fifth song, with its lyrics about natural and personal "spaces between"), Peart based his lyrics on a poem by Pye Dubois, a Canadian lyricist who also contributed to Rush's "Tom Sawyer" (*Moving Pictures*, 1981), "Force Ten" (*Hold Your Fire*, 1987), and "Test for Echo" (*Test for Echo*, 1996). Lifeson explains his inspiration for certain guitar sounds: "Pete Townshend [of the Who] can make an acoustic sound so heavy and powerful. I've always admired that. On 'Between Sun & Moon' there's a musical bridge before the solo that's very Who-ish." He described the song as a "tribute to the '60s," but he also enthused about early-1990s bands, such as Curve, Pearl Jam, and Alice in Chains ("Profile: Alex Lifeson" 1993).

Following up on "Ghost of a Chance" (*Roll the Bones*, 1991) and, to a lesser extent, *Counterparts'* song "Animate," Peart says of "Alien Shore" (the album's sixth song):

> I was thinking about these discussions among friends that I've had where, when we talk about gender differences or about racial differences, we can talk about them dispassionately because we were . . . generous, well-travelled people who counted all these different people among our friends and equals. I realize that these subjects are too dangerous in many cases to discuss because they are so freighted with prejudice and misunderstanding. I wanted to take that on and put it into a personal context of a conversation that "you and I are different but we don't have a problem with that." ("Counterparts" 1994)

The "busy" character of the music texturally parallels the song's particular slant on the complexity of sexual and racial differences: "We reject these narrow attitudes." The lyrics also reference U.S. contexts: "holding truths to be self-evident" and "electing each other president."

About "The Speed of Love" (seventh), Peart says:

> [The appearance of first-person lyrics] is a bit of a red herring almost. . . . For some of the songs, the situations are entirely invented, like "Cold Fire" [the tenth song] or "[The] Speed of Love." . . . I went through great pains with those songs to warm them up in different ways and to warm up the whole concept of our lives being dominated by chance. So, in this case, with the dualities, I didn't want to present just black and white themes. ("Counterparts" 1994)

Peart also suggests:

> "The Speed of Love" is kind of mid-tempo, a more sensitive rock song. [It] probably took me the longest [of the songs on *Counterparts*] to find just the right elements I wanted to have in a drum part.

What made it a challenge is that I wanted the feel and the transitions
between sections to be just right. I played [it] over and over, refining
it until I was satisfied. I don't think a listener will hear all the work
that went into that track. (Miller 1994)

Peart spent considerable time working out his drum parts, and the last
sentence here seems to suggest a slight frustration with the band's fans.
However, the interview took place in *Modern Drummer*, a U.S.-based
musician-oriented magazine for which Peart served as an adviser. Thus,
Peart probably meant that musician-fans (i.e., listener-drummers)
would be able to hear his "work."

The album also contains additional songs with emotional content.
The eighth song, "Double Agent," lurches among a number of textures
and rhythms. It also includes Lee's spoken voice sections, which stylistically reference the blues as opposed to the rap of "Roll the Bones" (*Roll
the Bones*, 1991). Peart also inserted elements from his reading:

"Wilderness of mirrors" is a phrase from T. S. Eliot's *Gerontion* and
was also applied by former CIA counter-intelligence chief James
Jesus Angleton to describe the world of espionage—hence the twist
on "Double Agent," reflecting the clandestine workings of dreams
and the subconscious. (*Counterparts* [Tour booklet] 1993–1994)

"Leave That Thing Alone" (ninth and Grammy nominated) functions as a sequel to the similar instrumental "Where's My Thing?" (*Roll
the Bones*, 1991). Its multisectional form and incorporation of synthesizers and funk-referencing rhythms somewhat recall its predecessor.

Like "The Speed of Love," "Cold Fire" (tenth of eleven) uses first-
person lyrics to address the topic of heterosexual relationships. Lifeson
describes the song as follows (*Counterparts* radio premiere broadcast,
1993): "I think there's a great balance between the romantic picture on
the one side, and how the music is sympathetic to those lyrics, and then
the other point of view, which is much colder." Peart explains his reluc-
tance to write love songs:

I think that love songs are not only dumb, they're also actively harm-
ful. They invent this fantasy that people expect their own relationships to live up to, and when they don't they result in divorces and
low self-esteem and sense of failure and all that, so it's not healthy.
Trying to express how a relationship really works, I invented charac-

ters and invented a situation and personalized it. Made it like a conversation between two people, of whom the woman is the smarter of the two, and made a complex little personal story. (Gehret 1994)

Peart took music, lyrics, *and* relationships seriously, so one might wish to differentiate his approach to love songs as "relationship songs," compared to rock music's much more common emphasis on "sex songs."

The album's closing anthem, "Everyday Glory" (eleventh), although not a love song, applies personalized situations to the idea of role models. As Peart puts it:

All we need is a good example from people. "Everyday Glory" contains that thought as well. That one spark of light to set an example is really the best thing that you can do. Being a parent myself, too, that's my law of parenthood. Number one: "don't warp them out" and number two: "set a good example." ("Counterparts" 1994, 37)

Thus, the song's sentiment reprises the main idea from the album's fourth song, "Nobody's Hero."

From 1990 to 1994, Rush's opening acts included the progressive-influenced rock, hard rock, and pop-rock bands and solo artists Mr. Big, Eric Johnson, Vinnie Moore, Primus, and Candlebox. Also, Rush's home shows at Maple Leaf Gardens paired them with major, somewhat younger, Canadian, heavy metal, and hard rock colleagues Voivod, the Tragically Hip, and I Mother Earth. The diversity of rock music reflected in such a field of opening acts then also influenced Rush as it entered the late 1990s. However, by 1996 the band had "done its duty" in supporting other bands and had a considerable amount of its own material to play (in two long sets). So, it stopped touring with opening acts starting in the fall of 1996.

8

"TO THE MARGIN OF ERROR"

Eclectic Rock, Tragedies and Sabbatical, and Return,
1996–2003

Rush released a new studio album about every year from 1974 to 1984 (ten albums) and every other year from 1985 to 1993 (five albums). For each album, the band averaged five to six months writing, arranging, rehearsing, and recording and six to seven months touring (plus frequent interviews). The band also assembled live albums in 1976, 1981, and 1989. There were also mostly studio compilation albums in 1978, 1990, and 1997: the non-chronologically-arranged discs *Retrospective I (1974–1980)* and *Retrospective II (1981–1987)*. From the early summer of 1994 until midfall of 1995, the band took a well-deserved seventeen-month break in order to pursue other activities. It would later take a much longer break, but for tragic, personal reasons.

Between *Counterparts* and its subsequent tour (1993–1994) and Rush's sixteenth studio album, *Test for Echo* (1996–1997), Neil Peart produced two Buddy Rich (1917–1987) tribute albums: *Burning for Buddy: A Tribute to the Music of Buddy Rich, Vol. 1* (1994) and *Burning for Buddy: A Tribute to the Music of Buddy Rich, Vol. 2* (1997). Various artists, including Peart and numerous additional rock and jazz drummers, recorded these at Bearsville Studios in central New York State. Rush engineer (1979–1982) and live (1998) and studio (2001–2002) coproducer Paul Northfield engineered the albums, and Rush's long-term album artist Hugh Syme created the covers. A video for each volume also appeared in 2000. Also in the mid-1990s, Peart wrote *The Masked Rider: Cycling in West Africa*. Hugh Syme designed the book's artwork. In 1995, Alex Lifeson made the "solo" album *Victor* (released in early 1996) with various non-Rush colleagues. Geddy Lee and his wife Nancy had a baby girl in 1994.

TEST FOR ECHO (1996)

In 1995–1996, the band reconvened to write and record its sixteenth studio album, *Test for Echo*. As with *Counterparts* (1993), it coproduced the album with UK producer Peter Collins and largely recorded it in Toronto. On the album, only brief sections of "Time and Motion," "Resist," and "Limbo" (the instrumental) use synthesizers or samplers more than incidentally. Moreover, unlike all six of the band's studio albums from 1984 to 1993, no external keyboardist or programmer receives credit on this album. Many songs instead feature Lifeson's elaborately layered guitar sounds to support a prominent, memorable vocal melody. Although Lee and Lifeson's music for this album tends to use technology even less than on Rush's albums from 1989 to 1993, Peart's lyrics nonetheless sometimes address technology. However, such lyrics tend toward ambivalence, thus suggesting a symbiosis with the album's stylistic undertaking. As for his drumming, in 1996 Peart released an instructional drumming video, *Neil Peart: A Work in Progress* (DCI). He based the video on his contributions to *Test for Echo* (1996) and around the reworking, circa 1994–1996, of his drumming technique based on input from jazz drummer and Buddy Rich associate Freddie Gruber. Hugh Syme created the video's cover design, which he based partly on his artwork for *Test for Echo*.

Hugh Syme's album cover for *Test for Echo* shows three tiny figures, presumably representing the members of the band. The Inuit traditionally used Inukshuks (meaning "in the image of man") in hunting practices and to mark trails and geographical directions. In Rush's context, this represents the band's long, complicated engagement with rock music. The CD's back cover technologically updates the front cover's ancient symbol with three large satellite dishes in the same Arctic tundra. The first page of the CD booklet features a digitally altered ancient map of the Northern Hemisphere (in Latin, but modified to refer to Rush). Each song gets a visual treatment:

- a photograph of a wolf howling at the full moon ("Test for Echo")
- an Inuit or Inuit-like artwork of a dogsled team ("Driven")
- the earth appears ripped in two; the album cover shows through ("Half the World")
- the northern lights ("The Color of Right")
- an artistically archaic globe and the coupling of two train cars ("Time and Motion")
- the lunar monolith from the 1968 film *2001: A Space Odyssey* ("Totem")
- adolescent pictures of aspiring rockers Peart, Lifeson, and Lee ("Dog Years"); a faint sketch of the cover's Inukshuk (an adolescent version of the eventual version?); dog shown wearing "Rush Limbo" dog tag (song no. 10,"Limbo," is instrumental)
- the skeleton of a sunken ship ("Virtuality"—the Internet as "mariners adrift")
- the cover's Inukshuk, now atop a mountain and with a "No-U-Turn" sign ("Resist")
- Inuit sculptors carving a rock sculpture; plus, carved onto a rock: "If you want something done right . . . just forget it" ("Carve Away the Stone")

The last (i.e., credits) page of the CD booklet includes a snowman family of three.

Syme also directed the textured-surface artwork of the two-CD Rush anthology, *Chronicles* (Mercury/Anthem, 1991). The cover of *Retrospective I (1974–1980)* (Mercury/Anthem, 1997) features an art gallery-like image, by another Canadian artist—Dan Hudson, of Syme's man-against-star cover for *2112* (1976). Syme provided a parallel, framed artwork of three fingerprints (one for each band member) for *Retrospective II (1981–1987)* (also Mercury/Anthem, 1997). Syme places a sweeper-janitor in both covers, but the custodian (probably representing Syme himself) only admires Hudson's (1974–1980) painting, not Syme's (1981–1987) painting. The CD booklets also include the relevant original album covers (by Syme, except for the first two) in frames elsewhere on the same gallery wall. Syme includes the

1974–1980 anthology cover, including Hudson's painting, as the last entry along the gallery wall in the 1981–1987 anthology—imagery that seems appropriate given that Rush often visited art galleries and museums in its concert tour cities. In a related vein, Rush agreed that Mercury Records could release a new anthology in 2003, a single CD that covered 1974 to 1987, but only if Mercury hired Hugh Syme to create the album art. There were also several later Rush anthologies of studio-recorded songs, in addition to many additional Rush live albums.

Test for Echo credits the words and music to Lee, Lifeson, and Peart, with the exception of the opening song, which it credits to Lee, Lifeson, Peart, and Dubois. Peart probably wrote or cowrote most of the lyrics, but Lee and/or Lifeson might have written or contributed to some of them. In fact, both wrote lyrics on several early Rush albums and on their 2000 and 1996 solo albums, respectively. The album's transcription folio retains the joint words/music authorship claim, as do all songs—even ones written before 1996—appearing on *Different Stages* (live, 1998).

"Test for Echo" (The Song)

Peart cowrote the lyrics of the album's opening title song, "Test for Echo," with occasional Rush collaborator Pye Dubois. The song addresses reality-based crime TV: "nail-biting 'hood boys in borrowed ties and jackets." The song also makes some reference to the 1995 O. J. Simpson murder trial ("the showcase trial on TV") that took place just as the band began to write the songs for this album. Musically, certain parts of the song recall the frantic tone of "Chain Lightning" from *Presto* (1989) and "Double Agent" from *Counterparts* (1993). The song contrasts its main moderate/cross-rhythmic main gesture of wide-ranging, undulating, and varied through modally mixed chords with a rhythmically complex second gesture that is narrow in range and somewhat frantic sounding, a cut-time/harmonically slower verse section, a claustrophobic- or paranoid-sounding chromatic ascent, and related material. These gestures, including some transpositions, underlie the song's various vocal and instrumental sections and encapsulate the lyrics' ambivalence toward society's simultaneous wide-eyed fascination and revulsion for the media. The song also seems to encapsulate "reality TV," perhaps especially the disturbingly popular show *Cops*.

The Rest of *Test for Echo*

The second song, "Driven," varies significantly in texture among its several sections. The verses feature a distorted progressive hard guitar riff that alternates among 4/4, 3/4, and 7/8 time signatures. The band's live performances of the song feature Lee's bass-guitar solo, which provides a sense of the riff's origin in jamming. (Live performances in 2002 also included film elements of the song's manic and humorous music video, featuring "little people" racing miniature race cars.) The studio version includes three tracks of bass guitar, and the song's bridge features strummed acoustic guitars. The chorus and the middle feature more mainstream rock style, the latter in a halftime feel: "Driven to the margin of error. Driven to the edge of control." Although not as texturally sparse, parts of this song thus musically and lyrically somewhat recall "Stick It Out" (*Counterparts*, 1993). Responding to an interviewer's comment about the band's continuing, partial interest in underlying funk- and groove-oriented playing, Lee self-effacingly describes the band's success as "about as funky as white Canadians get" (Dawdy 1996).

"Half the World" (third) provides a "camera eye," perhaps "satellite-cam," view of some of our world's complexities, such as "Half the world gives while the other half takes." Concerning the song's stylistic compromise of several Rush tendencies, Lee suggests:

> Rush is always torn between its more complex aggressive side and its softer side. Even though this song ["Half the World"] is not soft, it's melodic, so I put it in that other category. To me, this is one example where I think we were able to marry slightly edgier sound with that nice, melodic thing, so I was really pleased with this song. (*Test for Echo* [radio premiere broadcast] 1996)

Lee also says:

> "Half The World" is . . . a concise song without being wimpy or syrupy. It's got a little bit of everything: nice melody, and yet it's still aggressive. It's hard for us to write that kind of song, really. You'd have to go back to "Closer to the Heart" [*A Farewell to Kings*, 1977] to find an example of that. (Myers 1996, 39)

The older song applies the band's melodic/aggressive stylistic balance to espouse socioeconomic diversity among individuals (e.g., "You can be the captain, and I will draw the chart"). By comparison, "Half the World" applies this stylistic balance to macro/global contexts of sociopolitical intolerance, economic/industrial disparity, and postcolonialism. The song's video treats this more simply, with a fence separating Peart from Lee and Lifeson, which visually acknowledges the "Boys' Camp" manner in which the band composes its songs—written "separately together."

"The Color of Right" (fourth) suggests that goodness and truth become colored by rightness, by which Peart presumably means political correctness. Before 1996, Peart used British/Canadian spellings, such as "colour" and "honour." However, he probably felt compelled to fly in the face of his own conventions in such a song. In the last two lines of the chorus, Peart also applies concepts from physics to his sociological problematizing of rightness. In addition, the first verse refers to the narrator's own "sense of mission and the sense of what is right." Thus, the narrator even seems to implicate himself.

The opening/middle/ending instrumental section of "Time and Motion" (fifth) prominently features alternations between 5/4 and 12/8. In the verses, the band "smooths out" the oddity of this alternation into 6/4. The lyrics apply principles from science and nature to the human condition: "The mighty ocean dances with the moon. The silent forest echoes with the loon. . . . Time and motion. Live and love and dream. Eyes connect like interstellar beams." "Loon" refers to the northern lake bird so common in Canada, but it also suggests "loony" (derived from "lunatic") and/or the Canadian nickname of the nation's one-dollar coin: "loonie" (introduced in 1987 and featuring a loon). One of Peart's houses sits alongside a lake in Quebec, so he may have been thinking of a combination of at least two of the meanings (i.e., himself as "loony").

"Totem" (sixth) oddly embraces no religion by mentioning aspects of quite a few of them, such as Judeo-Christianity, Buddhism, Islam, Hinduism, paganism, and animism. The song similarly assembles contradictory musical styles, ironically quoting the title of the African American spiritual "Swing Low, Sweet Chariot" and also using vaguely Celtic music. Of "Totem," Lifeson says:

> I created a soundscape by using harmonics with a kind of Celtic melody over it that's quite distant. In the song, in terms of dynamics, it's a really beautiful shift. Listening to it in cans [i.e., with headphones], there's this line "angels and demons inside my head" that was very visual to me. It's almost angelic. You can sort of see this imagery swirling around." (Myers 1996, 35, 38)

The song also implicates the mass media in propagating religiosity: "Media messiahs preying on my fears. Pop culture prophets playing in my ears." This suggests something along the lines of pop culture as a religion *and* an "opiate of the masses."

Of "Dog Years" (seventh) Peart says that he wrote the whimsical lyrics:

> Right when we got together . . . after quite a long break apart. We did a little celebrating the first night, and the following day I was a bit the worse for wear. . . . I sat down all muzzy-headed like that and started trying to stitch words together. . . . "Dog Years" . . . came out of that kind of mentality, and born of observations over the years too, of looking at my dog thinking, "What's going through his brain?" and I would think, "Just a low-level zzzzz static—'food,' 'walk'—the basic elemental things." When I look at my dog that's how I see his brainwaves moving. . . . I say, "I don't think he's thinking about too much." (*Test for Echo* [radio premiere broadcast] 1996)

"Virtuality" (eighth) addresses the Internet. The chorus seems almost annoyingly optimistic, yet the verses and bridges suggest the artificiality of such a virtual reality: "Astronauts in the weightlessness of pixellated space exchange graffiti with a disembodied race." Especially at phrase ends during the song's verses, Lee's bass notes contradict those of Lifeson's guitar. These elements further enhance the artificiality, as does Lifeson's chromatic opening riff, which also underlies the verses and parts of the bridges. The chorus shifts into a more "power pop" style and an unambiguous minor key. Earlier Rush songs, such as "2112" (*2112*, from 1976) and "Superconductor" (*Presto*, 1989), suggest that the band probably means such tonal, textural, and genre "clarifications" ironically. Just before the release of *Test for Echo* (1996), Peart complained about the Internet in a "Note from Neil" in *Modern Drummer* (August 1996). For about fifteen years, Peart responded by postcard or brief response to thousands of letters forwarded to him by the magazine. However, the ease of communication facilitated by the Internet (he called it the "World-Wide GossipNet" and the "Inter-thingy") meant that he could no longer continue with his "little secret."

The ninth song, "Resist," suggests a waltz, through its near-pervasive use of triple meter. Musically, the song suggests an origin in a folklike, voice-with-acoustic-guitar context. A diatonic piano melody and Lee's prominent vocal harmonies (often modal sounding, in fourths instead of sixths or thirds) add to the song's folklike character. Lee sometimes sings rhythmically, emotionally, and wordlessly on the syllable "la." Led Zeppelin's Robert Plant similarly uses a cappella "la" sections in "Black Dog" (*Led Zeppelin IV*, 1971) and "The Ocean" (*Houses of the Holy*, 1973) as textural/rhythmic pauses within songs otherwise based on highly complex hard rock riffs. Although Rush derived much of its 1971–1975 inspiration from Led Zeppelin, Lee's wordless sections in "Resist" function as natural extensions of the song's existing folklike, emotional tone and, particularly, its waltz-like triple meter.

The lyrics of "Resist" address temptation and compromise in the context of moderate individualism and agnosticism, such as from the song's chorus: "I can learn to resist anything but temptation. I can learn to coexist with anything but pain. I can learn to compromise anything but my desires. I can learn to get along with all the things I can't explain." The song's middle section provides a contrasting, even less rocklike, texture in 4/4 time. It features Lee's solo voice (i.e., without any harmony) and Lifeson's sparsely strummed acoustic guitar, with Peart joining in with subtle crescendos on a cymbal. Rush embraced the folklike essence of "Resist" during the band's 2002 concert tour. Lee and Lifeson performed the song in an "unplugged" style on stools near the front of the stage. Both played acoustic guitars, but only Lee sang. The incorporation of such a one-song "mini acoustic set" served to demonstrate something of the kinder, gentler, emotional side of Rush that the band often buried in its elaborate musicianship. Wholly related to this, the live performances of "Resist" also provided Neil Peart with a brief respite after his elaborate, highly virtuosic jazz-rock drum solo. Rush's acoustic version of "Resist" combined the song's *compositional* origins with a partial rest for Lee and Lifeson and a real rest for Peart. The band played "Resist" in a normal rock style during its 1996–1997 tour and again during certain later tours.

"Limbo" (tenth), an instrumental, allowed the band to indulge in nonseriousness for a few additional moments near the end of the album. The song's title implies Rush Limbaugh, although the song has nothing to do with the U.S. populist conservative. This represents the first time that Rush itself incorporated a near-pun on the band's name. It resisted calling the song "Rush Limbo," but the CD artwork for the lyrics of "Dog Years" shows a dog with a tag bearing that name. Perhaps inspired by "Resist," this, the band's fifth studio instrumental, occasionally includes wordless vocals (e.g., "Ah"). In a humorous vein, it also includes several samples from Bobby "Boris" Pickett's early-1960s Halloween dance novelty classic "The Monster Mash." (The original song capitalized on the Mashed Potato, an early-1960s dance fad.) In "Limbo," Rush avoids Bobby Pickett's imitation of the classic horror film actor Boris Karloff in favor of occasional samples from the song's gurgling laboratory sounds, Dracula's complaint "Whatever happened to my Transylvania Twist" and Igor's enthusiastic "mmm . . . mash good! . . . mmm."

The title of "Carve Away the Stone," the closing (eleventh) song, on the surface seems to suggest something along the lines of the Inuit stone-carving photograph shown in the CD's liner notes. However, it actually presents a version of the Sisyphus myth: "You can roll that stone to the top of the hill, drag your ball and chain behind you. You can carry that weight with an iron will, or let the pain remain behind you. Chip away the stone. Make the burden lighter, if you must roll that rock alone." Verse 2 approaches the punishment meted out to Sisyphus from a more modern viewpoint: unsuccessfully trying to escape from the psychological weight of acts committed. Chorus 2 "ups the ante" from merely chipping the stone to carving something of oneself into it. After a guitar solo, verse 3 combines aspects of the first two verses. Chorus 3 then tells Sisyphus, or his modern equivalent, to roll the stone away completely—the narrator wants room to get working on his *own* stone.

Musically, the song frequently varies from among a number of different time signatures (4/4, 5/4, 6/4, 7/4) and, similarly, tonal implications. The opening/verse chord progression introduces a "cross relation" that anticipates the tonal area of verse 3. That verse also includes the cross relation, now up a tone, but the following prechorus/chorus drops immediately back to other keys. On the other hand, the song's final repeated instrumental section (with its various extended chords) precludes any ultimate tonal stability, as does its final chord. These elements parallel the uneven (asymmetrical) distribution of energies suggested in the lyrics. Also, this concluding song's verse-phrase closing chords reflect the tonal areas of about half the songs on the album. Rolling a large stone up a hill or dealing with psychological issues ("weight") takes considerable time and effort, and then the cycle might very well begin again immediately.

Around the time of the later parts of the *Test for Echo* tour, the U.S. alternative rock band Pavement referenced the disparity between Lee's speaking voice (baritone) and singing voice (countertenor) in its song "Stereo" (*Brighten the Corners*, 1997):

> What about the voice of Geddy Lee; how did it get so high?
> I wonder if he speaks like an ordinary guy.
> [Other voice:] I know him, and he does!
> [First voice:] And you're my fact-checking cuz.

Rush found the reference humorous and included the song in its concert warm-up tapes.

However, Rush's well-entrenched album/touring cycle was tragically interrupted.

TRAGEDIES AND SABBATICAL

Between July 4, 1997 (the end of the *Test for Echo* tour) and September 11, 2000, a great deal changed for Rush—especially for Neil Peart. His only child, Selena, died in a single-car accident on August 10, 1997 (several weeks before she would have started university), and his spouse, Jacqueline Taylor, died of cancer in June of 1998. Peart retired from music making, lived for extended periods in England and Barbados (with his wife before she died), and then traveled fifty-five thousand miles by motorcycle throughout Canada, the United States, Mexico, and Belize. He wrote hundreds of letters (especially to his recently imprisoned pot-smuggling best friend), read numerous fiction and non-fiction books, and wrote part of one book and most of another (the latter published in 2002). He also convinced himself to start dating (after over twenty years), started playing the drums again, met his future second wife (California native Carrie Nuttall) in Los Angeles, got married near Santa Barbara, and moved to his wife's adopted home of Santa Monica. Peart continued to keep at least one house in Canada.

During Peart's period of mental and emotional recovery (late 1997 to the end of 2000), Geddy Lee and Alex Lifeson kept musically busy and, to a certain extent, kept Rush alive. That included putting together the band's fourth live album, *Different Stages* (1998), comprising two CDs of performances from recent tours (mostly in the United States, but also some songs from Canada and the UK), plus a third CD of a "classic" Rush show from the UK in 1978.

Hugh Syme's cover for *Different Stages* shows three differently colored components of a child's Tinkertoy. The separate components presumably refer to the individual band members, and the toy itself refers to the band. The inner packaging refers to the combination of mid-1990s and late-1970s recordings by placing humorous 1990s images of Lee and Lifeson (along with fictitious 1998 concert posters) into a photo otherwise apparently taken outside London's Hammersmith Odeon just before a 1978 Rush show. Unusually, the CD package uses a format entirely made of paper, and one disc also includes software for a computer-based arts program called "Clusterworks," by Japanese artist and Rush fan Hisashi Hoda. (Rush enjoyed a substantial following in Japan.) The album booklet includes a photo collage of numerous Rush items from between the early 1970s and 1997, thus substantially expanding on the concert photographs provided in the packaging materials of the band's three earlier live albums.

After Peart's dual tragedies, even Lifeson did not play a guitar at all for over a year. However, he is also a painter and a licensed pilot, so he may have focused on those things instead. In 1997, he contributed his version of "The Little Drummer Boy" to *Merry Axemas*, a "guitar hero" Christmas album. Then, in starting to come out of the band's sabbatical, in 1999 Lee and Lifeson provided a version of "O Canada" for the soundtrack album of *South Park: Bigger, Longer & Uncut*. In 2000, Lifeson also made a multitrack, guitar-based theme for the TV sci-fi series *Andromeda*. Meanwhile, Lee made a solo album, *My Favourite Headache* (2000). It includes a wide variety of styles, not all of them associated with Rush. The album includes eleven songs, musically co-written with Canadian musician-songwriter Ben Mink and featuring alternative rock drummer Matt Cameron. The album features an elaborate, paper-based design similar to that of *Different Stages*, and its lyrics were provided on a website. Around the same time, Rush received a star on Canada's Walk of Fame (in Toronto, in 1999) and won "Most Important Canadian Musicians of All Time" (ahead of No. 2, the Band, and No. 3, the Tragically Hip) in a 2000 poll taken by the Canadian music e-journal *JAM!* A little later, in 2001, Rush's former record label, Mercury, also released a DVD update of its Rush music video collection, *Chronicles* (1991). Like its VHS predecessor, it covers material from 1977 to 1987.

VAPOR TRAILS (2002)

In January of 2001, Rush reconvened to write and record its seventeenth studio album, *Vapor Trails*. The band recorded the album at Toronto's Reaction Studios, coproducing it with its earlier engineer, Paul Northfield. Finally, on March 29, 2002, the band released its first new song in five and a half years: "One Little Victory." The album followed on May 14. *Vapor Trails* (2002) reverts to the usual procedure of Lee and Lifeson credited with the music and Peart credited with the words. Some of the album's songs, such as "One Little Victory" and "Freeze," somewhat evoke the band's early-1980s progressive hard semi-individualism, but "Ceiling Unlimited," "How It Is," and others appear somewhat inspired by much more recent, guitar-jangly Britpop. Much of the music also inscribes emotional resonances hardly heard in Rush's earlier music. This is not surprising, given the tumultuous circumstances of Neil Peart's life between 1997 and 2000. Moreover, by 2002 Peart had read books and articles by hundreds of fiction and nonfiction writers, including ancient and Middle English mythology; nineteenth-century classic novels; modern and contemporary North American, European, and world literature; literary travelogues (including London, Steinbeck, and Kerouac); and writings about psychology, science, nature, birds, art, cars, and motorcycles. He had also written numerous articles and several books.

Hugh Syme's cover for *Vapor Trails* depicts a stylized, painted comet. The comet's body seems to contain shadows and distorted faces, perhaps phantoms. The song "Vapor Trail," an analogy for fading memories, inspired not only the album title but also these images. The grammatically plural version suggests that each of the album's thirteen songs serves as a vapor trail. In the artwork, the comet's trail (tail?) carries over on the rear artwork of the CD booklet. When one fully opens the booklet, the comet appears with an extended trail across the front and back cover. When one sets the booklet in place in the CD packaging (and the disc itself is absent), the trail connects to a similar one on the disc inlay. Inside the CD booklet and on the album's website, Syme pairs the lyrics for each of the thirteen songs with a drawing of a suitable tarot card. The song "Peaceable Kingdom" refers to tarot cards. Some of the song-card associations fit better than others, but the overall effect gives a sense of rationalism challenged by uncontrollable forces. Although otherwise a "rational-scientific-sceptic," Peart reports that his interest in tarot cards dates to a reading he had in Venice Beach, California, while on a date in May 1999 (Peart 2002, 338).

"One Little Victory"

In "One Little Victory," the opening song of *Vapor Trails*, Alex Lifeson contributes heavy electric-guitar riffs (though often layered with "heavy acoustics"), the rhythmic motion of which also recalls his funk/groove experiments in music from between 1989 and 1993. The song tonally centers on E, primarily minor inflected but sometimes touching on Phrygian (or modified blues scale), pentatonic, mixolydian, and major, thus making the precise number of "tonal areas" difficult to pinpoint. This recalls Rush's modally mixed approach of the early 1980s, in which the band harmonically bridged the areas that it also bridged stylistically: blues rock, hard rock, heavy metal, progressive rock, and post-punk. The inclusion of heavy acoustic guitars recalls the Who, one "classic rock" band that all three members of Rush cited as an early influence.

As in many Rush songs, Geddy Lee plays an athletically leaping bass part in certain sections of "One Little Victory." In addition, he often sings higher than on most of the band's several dozen studio tracks from the 1990s. This suggests a coming to terms with the fact that many people, especially casual fans, expect him to sing this way. On the other hand, Lee sings in his natural chest voice for certain parts of the song, especially the first half of each verse, and he also experiments with changing the way he uses his countertenor and falsetto singing styles. In this and several other songs on *Vapor Trails*, Lee sometimes "flips" into falsetto by leap and by incorporating a slight timbral shift, more like in rhythm and blues, pop, or grunge. "One Little Victory" also features numerous vocal overdubs, along with subtle octave multitracking. These produce an almost "baroque" effect and also reflect some of the textures achieved on Lee's solo album *My Favourite Headache* (2000). Such experiments expanded the less pervasive use of vocal overdubs that Lee applied to the band's studio albums from the mid-1980s to *Test for Echo* (1996).

Throughout *Vapor Trails*, Lee's extensive vocal textures function as organic replacements for the synthesizer/sampler sounds he applied to much of the band's music between 1982 and 1987 and to a lesser extent between 1989 and 1996. As with certain 1980s Rush songs that proved difficult to play live (because of the number of synthesizers and samplers used on the recordings), Lee suggested that "Stars Look Down" may feature too many vocal overdubs to play the song live.

During "One Little Victory," Neil Peart often plays an underlying, "snappy," beat-anticipating drum pattern, yet the texture and density vary a number of times throughout. The song features numerous rhythmic complexities but almost none of the band's earlier predilection for asymmetrical time signatures (7/8, 5/4, etc.). The song invokes something like heavy metal "headbanging," but in a very peculiar Rush idiom. Indeed, one of the song's rhythms clearly evokes the short-long-short-long "swagger" rhythm of the band's 1981 song "Tom Sawyer." Peart's lyrics perfectly encapsulate Rush's moderate individualism of the 1980s and beyond, and the band thus also chose to open the album with this song. In March/April of 2002, Rush's website played "One Little Victory" continuously for several weeks, and rock radio stations added the song to their playlists more often than any other. Musically and lyrically, "One Little Victory" demonstrates the reasons for many rock critics never having come to terms with Rush. However, the reasons for Rush's influence on Primus and on other 1990s, alternative, progressive metal, and post-progressive bands ("musicians' musicians") certainly also hold for this song.

In a similar vein, the album's final song, "Out of the Cradle," ends with sung repetitions of the words "endlessly rocking." The members of Rush may not have intended this as humorous, but it nonetheless evokes the band's ongoing paradoxical status somewhere between "classic rock" and "contemporary rock." To complicate this even further, another song recalls "classic" Rush even more than "One Little Victory." "Freeze, Part IV of 'Fear'" with its complicated/shifting time signatures, provides an unexpected continuation of Neil Peart's 1981–1984 "Fear Trilogy"—"Witch Hunt," "The Weapon," and "The Enemy Within."

The Rest of *Vapor Trails*

Some of the thirteen songs on *Vapor Trails* (2002) suggest influences from a more pop-rock direction than is usual for Rush, including 1990s Britpop and, to a lesser extent, 1960s folk rock. This more "pop"-oriented style includes an emphasis on stepwise tunefulness, jangly (though generally still heavy) guitars, Lee's close vocal harmonies (often in "modal" parallel notes), and, in some songs, wordless vocalizing. For example, the band features such elements in "Ceiling Unlimited," "Ghost Rider," "How It Is," "Vapor Trail," "Sweet Miracle," and "Nocturne." The three songs discussed above, "One Little Victory," "Freeze," and "Out of the Cradle," fit more closely with Rush's post-1981 tempered individualism. They also fit with the band's continued interest in a somewhat consistent and aggressive progressive hard rock fusion. On the other hand, all three songs also feature some close vocal harmonies and wordless vocalizing. Positioned first, twelfth, and thirteenth (i.e., last), these songs provide a frame for the unusually high percentage of personal songs on much of the rest of the album. Four of the album's most beautiful songs, "Peaceable Kingdom," "The Stars Look Down," "Secret Touch," and "Earthshine" (balancing the album at positions 4, 5, 8, and 9 of 13), lyrically and musically combine the two tendencies.

Some of Peart's lyrics on *Vapor Trails*, especially "Ghost Rider" but also aspects of "How It Is," "Ceiling Unlimited," "Secret Touch," and "Vapor Trail," at least partly refer to his personal tragedies of 1997–1998 and/or his subsequent healing process. In addition, Peart details in his three-page,"Album Bio" press release for *Vapor Trails* (Universal Music Canada, 2002); it may also have been reprinted in the tour book, but the original was in the press release:

> I can trace some interesting sources for particular lines, like Walt Whitman in "Out of the Cradle" and Thomas Wolfe in "How It Is" ("foot upon the stair, shoulder to the wheel") and "Ceiling Unlimited" (Wolfe's title *Of Time and the River* and looking at a map of the

Mississippi Delta suggested the "winding like an ancient river" lines). "Ceiling Unlimited" also offers a playful take on Oscar Wilde's reversal of the Victorian lament, "drink is the curse of the working class" ["if culture is the curse of the thinking class"]. Joseph Conrad's *Victory* gave the "secret touch on the heart" line. "There is never love without pain" [also in "Secret Touch"] echoed from my own experience and the novel *Sister of My Heart*, by Chitra Banerjee Divakaruni, and W. H. Auden and Edward Abbey (*Black Sun*) influenced certain lines in "Vapor Trail."

Other songs, especially "Earthshine" and "Sweet Miracle" but perhaps also "Nocturne," more strongly suggest Peart's renewed lease on life. "Peaceable Kingdom," with its burning tower tarot card imagery in the CD booklet, seems to refer to the ethos of post–September 11, 2001. Peart suggests influences on these as well:

An article in the magazine *Utne Reader* called "What Do Dreams Want?" contributed to my ideas in "Nocturne" (as well as the enigmatic mantra, "the way out is the way in," for "Secret Touch"), and I was also struck by a psychologist's approach to analysis and dream interpretation, "without memory or desire" [also in "Nocturne"].

The nineteenth-century Quaker folk artist, Edward Hicks, painted no [fewer] than sixty versions of the same biblical scene, "Peaceable Kingdom" [the title of one of the album's songs, originally slated as the album's instrumental], and the tarot card "The Tower" [associated with "Peaceable Kingdom" in the CD booklet] seemed a chilling reflection of the events of September 11, 2001. A series of works by Canadian painter Paterson Ewen helped to inspire "Earthshine," and the title of a novel by A. J. Cronin, *The Stars Look Down* (which I've yet to read), seemed to express a fitting view of an uncaring universe. ("Album Bio")

Peart's literary influences reflect his relatively serious take on the world. However, they also indicate his combination of influences from various nineteenth- and twentieth-century figures from the United States, Europe, and Canada and from a variety of nonfiction.

In his *Vapor Trails* "Album Bio," Peart, author of several books and numerous articles, explains the renewed creative process:

> Sometimes a developing song seemed to lose momentum, or our *faith* (the critical force), and was abandoned, but that had always been our version of "natural selection."
>
> Once I had the reassurance of knowing that some of the lyrics were *working*, and had a feel for the musical context, I carried on with the lyric writing. And switching to my "drummer" hat, now that I had some song sketches to work on I started spending a few nights a week creating and refining drum parts, playing along to the still-evolving arrangements of music and vocals as my guide. [Guitarist] Alex [Lifeson] was my personal producer and recording engineer, as he had been for this phase of many past albums. ("Album Bio")

This "natural selection" means that Rush could fully determine the structure of most of its new music by the end of the refinement period of the compositional process.

Despite Rush's lengthy sabbatical (late 1997 to the end of 2000) and the comparatively long period of time to make the album *Vapor Trails* (2002), the band's renewed compositional approach and touring schedule resembled its earlier activities. However, the band's new music struck a more consistent emotional chord, probably due to Peart's family tragedies of 1997–1998 and his subsequent personal renewal—such as extensive traveling, reading, and writing in addition to remarrying and resuming as a powerful drummer-lyricist.

On *Vapor Trails*, Lee's strong vocal melodies (often incorporating countertenor), ornate vocal harmonies, elaborate bass playing, and avoidance of keyboards reflect a deepening of the band's traditional lyrics/music "back-and-forth." Lifeson's prominent electric guitars, with extensive riffs, layering, solos, and "hard alternative" influences, also look forward while simultaneously looking back. On the other hand, the album engendered some controversy, as many people felt that its recording levels were much too high, resulting in a "distorted" quality throughout. Several songs were initially remixed for a compilation album, but then the entire album was remixed in 2013. The "remix" version of the album does not rework the structure of any of its songs, though. It only remixes the volume, stereo placement, and similar elements of their audio design. So, it is not a "remix" album in the usual sense of merging in unexpected styles or artists. Shortly after *Vapor Trails*, Rush released the chronological single-disc *The Spirit of Radio: Greatest Hits 1974–1987*. In 2003, the band then released its next (fifth) live album, *Rush in Rio*, which was recorded and filmed (for its video version) in front of forty thousand fans at Rio de Janeiro, Brazil's Estádio do Maracanã in 2002. It includes Neil Peart's Grammy-nominated drum solo, "O Baterista" ("The Drummer"), and the video version won the 2004 Juno Award for Music DVD of the Year.

On December 31, 2003, Alex Lifeson and members of his family attended a New Year's Eve party at the Ritz-Carlton hotel in Naples, Florida. Lifeson owned a home in the area, and music for the event was being provided by the band of Nat King Cole's younger brother, Freddy. Lifeson and his thirty-three-year-old son, Justin Zivojinovich, got into an altercation with security guards about Justin's somewhat rambunctious behavior (e.g., wanting to sing onstage). The Collier County Sheriff's Department was called in, and things escalated, including pushing and shoving, excessive force, Lifeson's nose being broken, the multiple use of Tasers, and the arrest of Lifeson and his son. They were released on bail. In 2005, a plea agreement was arranged so that they would avoid jail time by pleading no contest to the first-degree misdemeanor charge of resisting arrest without violence. Lifeson also pursued a civil case against the hotel and the sheriff's department. In 2008, he received an out-of-court settlement from the hotel for "their incredibly discourteous, arrogant and aggressive behaviour of which I had never experienced in thirty years of travel." The incident in Naples was clearly an anomaly, though, for the members of Rush have been best known outside of its music for reading, bicycling, sports, visiting museums, contributing to charities, and so on.

9

"SOME WILL BE REWARDED"

Getting to the Rock and Roll Hall of Fame, 2004–2013

In the 2000s and 2010s, Rush released several new studio albums, toured internationally, compiled a number of live albums and videos, put out various anthologies of its earlier work, and appeared on mainstream TV shows and in major-release movies. Despite the band's tenuous position vis-à-vis rock critics (many of them had disliked most of its music over the years), Rush increasingly came to be recognized as major, influential artists of the past several decades. In 2012—for the first time in the band's thirty-eight-year professional career—*Rolling Stone* magazine featured Rush in a cover story. Then, in 2013, the band was inducted into the Rock and Roll Hall of Fame. Its next two studio albums were *Snakes & Arrows* (2007) and *Clockwork Angels* (2012).

FEEDBACK (2004, REVISITING THE BAND'S EARLY COVER SONGS)

In 2004, Rush delved remarkably far into its past by releasing a modest, "thirtieth-anniversary," eight-song CD: *Feedback*. The album features "psychedelic" artwork (evocative of the late 1960s), and the music comprises cover versions of songs that the band members had performed as teenagers in the late 1960s and very early 1970s—"Summertime Blues" (Eddie Cochran, in the cover version by Blue Cheer), "Heart Full of

Soul" (the Yardbirds), "The Seeker" (the Who), "For What It's Worth" (Buffalo Springfield), "Shapes of Things" (the Yardbirds), "Mr. Soul" (Buffalo Springfield), "Seven and Seven Is" (Love), and "Crossroads" (in Cream's version of the Robert Johnson song). Even "Rush-resistant" rock critics found themselves pleasantly surprised that the band had gone this route, instead of putting together a ponderous boxed set from its own three decades of material. The album is not usually counted as a Rush "studio album."

R30 (2005, FROM RUSH'S THIRTIETH-ANNIVERSARY 2004 WORLD TOUR)

Rush's live albums functioned as anthologies to supplement the ones also released of selected (mostly) studio songs: the two-disc, nonchronological *Gold* (2006, of music from 1974 to 1987) and the single-disc *Retrospective III (1989–2008)* (2009, of Atlantic-era music from 1989 to 2008). The band's fifth and sixth live albums (and videos), *Rush in Rio* (2003) and *R30* (2005, of 2004's thirtieth-anniversary world tour), respectively, allowed the band to acknowledge its important secondary audience outside of North America. *R30* was recorded and filmed at Frankfurt, Germany's 13,500-seat Festhalle in 2004.

Rush's 2004 tour included numerous visual elements, an opening instrumental overture of riffs derived from six songs from the 1970s, and performances of several of the cover songs from *Feedback* (2004). It also included opening and closing taped comedy elements involving veteran TV comedian Jerry Stiller, who is undoubtedly best known as the neurotic father of George Costanza on *Seinfeld*. Rush concerts draw a combination of "hard-core" musician-fans, other fans of the band, and casual observers, so the band probably intended these elements as added-value entertainment for its still-evolving audience.

R30's disc 1 (130 min.) was recorded with fourteen high-definition cameras in digital surround sound and wide screen. The set's deluxe edition also includes two audio CDs containing the same music. The band performs its album-oriented rock (AOR) music live so that it conforms very closely to the original studio versions. Its music draws upon various guitars and basses, numerous effects pedals, bass pedal instruments, synthesizer keyboards, triggered samples, and Peart's extremely large array of drums and percussion. A revolving platform is used to alter the latter's configuration, such as during the drum solo, "Der Trommler" ("The Drummer"). Rush concerts feature a variety of visual and lighting effects, and *R30* includes colored patterns, spotlights, dry-ice "smoke," lasers, and audience sweeps. It also included many stage-rear-screen projections: images based on the band's album-cover art (most by Hugh Syme); live and archive images of the three band members; computer-produced visual effects patterns; selected elements borrowed and/or updated from several of the band's music videos; and a humorous midshow animation featuring a Godzilla-like dragon and a trio of Rush "bobble-heads."

R30's disc 2 contains five band-member interviews from 1979 to 2002. They cover Rush's nonmainstream arena rock, "democracy of three" ideals, and its history of fostering a dedicated core audience that tolerates the band's individualist experiments. The disc also includes a "live" video (actually synced-to-studio recording) of a 1975 Rush song, two live performances from the mid-1970s U.S. TV show *Don Kirshner's Rock Concert*, four onstage live videos from about 1979, an early live sound check of "The Spirit of Radio" (a month or two before it was first recorded in the autumn of 1979), a pair of live song performances from major Canadian multiartist events in 2003 and 2005, and some fairly trivial "hidden" bonus materials (referred to as "Easter eggs"). The 1970s interviews and performances usefully document that period's long hairstyles, silk shirts revealing hairy chests, bell-bottomed pants, and even the occasional cape. In a further nod to the band's past, in 2006 Rush released *Replay X 3*, comprising DVD videos of three earlier live tours that had previously been released on VHS and laser disc: *Exit . . . Stage Left* (1982), *Grace under Pressure* (1985), and *A Show of Hands* (1989). The first and third of those are similar in content to the band's identically named second and third live albums.

TV SHOWS, MOVIES, AND SO ON

In 2003, Lifeson had guest-starred as himself as a kidnapping victim in an episode of the popular Canadian cable TV comedy series *Trailer Park Boys*. In 2005, during a major, televised Asian tsunami fund-raising event in Canada, the show's character Bubbles (Mike Smith) joined

Rush and Barenaked Ladies' Ed Robertson in a performance of the band's 1977 song "Closer to the Heart." In 2006, quotations from Rush's 1980 song "The Spirit of Radio" were then used as a kind of "theme song" for *Trailer Park Boys: The Movie*. Lifeson also had a cameo in that movie as a traffic cop, and he then had a more substantial one as an undercover vice squad officer (in drag) in 2009's *Trailer Park Boys: Countdown to Liquor Day*. Also in 2006, Neil Peart appeared on the Canadian comedy show *The Rick Mercer Report*, talking about his cycling and motorcycle rides between tour cities and while "on sabbatical." He also jammed with Mercer on adjacent drum kits. In the same year, Peart released his book *Roadshow: Landscape with Drums; A Concert Tour by Motorcycle*.

Rush also continued to be quite popular in the United States into the 2000s. Peart's drumming prowess was referred to in the 2003 mainstream movie *School of Rock*. In 2007, he provided voice-overs for the film version of the popular animated TV children's show *Aqua Teen Hunger Force*. More importantly, in 2008 Rush made appearances on the late-night TV show *The Colbert Report*, interviewed by Stephen Colbert and then also playing its 1981 song "Tom Sawyer." Also, in 2009 the band was featured prominently in the movie *I Love You, Man*. It features the band's "man-cave-suitable" music (air guitar, air drumming, etc.) and also plays up the stereotypical scenario of closely bonding males dragging along a skeptical girlfriend to a Rush concert. During its 2010–2011 tour, the band incorporated a related, spinoff, backstage comedy video, featuring Geddy Lee and the movie's two main actors, Paul Rudd and Jason Segel. In 2010, Rush was also the subject of a Canadian-made, major-release, critically well-received, and Grammy-nominated documentary: *Rush: Beyond the Lighted Stage*. The movie won the 2011 Juno Award for Music DVD of the Year. Also, starting in 2003, many of Rush's releases—especially DVD and Blu-ray discs of live performances—were also co-released in the United States on Rounder Records.

SNAKES & ARROWS (2007)

In late 2006 and early 2007, Rush recorded its eighteenth studio album of original music. The band coproduced it with Grammy

Award–winning producer/musician Nick Raskulinecz, and it was re-corded in upstate New York and mixed in Los Angeles. The title of *Snakes & Arrows* is presumably meant to conflate two expressions: "snakes & ladders" (the classic children's game, more widely known as "chutes and ladders" in the United States) and "slings & arrows," from the "To be or not to be" soliloquy in Shakespeare's *Hamlet*. The band had already referenced another expression from that soliloquy ("To sleep, perchance to dream . . .") in a section title within its 1978 instru-mental work, "La Villa Strangiato." The hybrid quote is actually used in the album's second song, "Armor and Sword." *Snakes & Arrows* con-tains a number of subtle references to Rush's past, both musically and lyrically. In a sense, the band seemed quite willing by 2007 to come to terms with its own legacy. Related to that, the album's American copro-ducer, Nick Raskulinecz, became a well-known rock producer in the 2000s (especially for the Foo Fighters), but he had grown up with and been a fan of Rush's earlier music.

"Far Cry"

On the album as a whole, Peart's lyrics often vacillate between positive and negative conditions and/or look forward and backward simultane-ously. The opening song, "Far Cry," does those things as well. The song somewhat recalls the cynical approach to the Internet of "Virtuality" (from 1996's *Test for Echo*), but it generalizes things a bit more by implying that communications and ambition can be in vain, because there are crazy people to fend off and obstacles to overcome. It's not possible to control everything; fortune ebbs and flows like the tide, sometimes you feel like you're "on top of the world," but other times it's "falling in" on you. The song's message is ultimately positive, though, because even though you go through hard times, you can always "get back on." "Far Cry" begins with a heavy, insistent, lurching, chordal rhythm in which it is difficult to identify the time signature. Throughout the song, the introductory lurching pattern is always followed by a "look back," by using the jazz-like (seventh and eleventh) extended chord of "Hemispheres" (1978) as a "stop-time" transition point into the song's verses, which then also resume aspects of rhythmic complexity. The verses are much more flowing and riff based than the song's lurching introduction, but some of their phrases drop a beat. That provides a less extreme approach to "odd rhythms" than the "micro-additive" ones (7/8, 5/4, etc.) that Rush had often explored in the late 1970s and early 1980s, such as in "Hemispheres" and on *Moving Pictures*. However, the tactic did return the band to something more like the kind of "nerdy playfulness" with which it had earlier been so powerfully associated.

"Armor and Sword"

The album's second song, "Armor and Sword," begins with hard rock, electric-guitar-based music that previews its later, riff-based prechorus. The song's verses, though, are in a triple-beat (waltz-like), soft rock and acoustic-guitar-based style, and verse 1 references the "snakes and arrows" that have been able to cut you since childhood. The song's title is taken from a line in its first prechorus, referring to one's defenses ("armor") surfacing instead as anger ("sword"). The chorus remains in hard rock style, but it is more open and chordal than the riff-oriented prechorus. The "hybrid" style thus parallels the ideological viewpoint of the chorus's lyrics, that "no one gets to their heaven without a fight." The song combines hard and soft rock styles, as well as contrasting time signatures. Such compromises thus musically espouse the psychological benefits that come from going through rewarding struggles instead of merely vacillating between defense and anger.

The Rest of *Snakes & Arrows*

"Workin' Them Angels" (the album's third song) also balances looking backward and forward. It is a semiautobiographical, stylistically hard rock recollection by Neil Peart of his various travels, merged with reminiscences of his activities as a musician: driving away to the east while looking to the past, a desert road, a factory town, a wave of music (thus referencing the band's 1980 album *Permanent Waves*), and riding (e.g., bicycles) and driving (e.g., motorcycles) and living "close to the edge" (thus requiring the intervention of angels). Later parts of the song also reference the memory of a "wounded city," a "moving picture" (referencing the band's 1981 album *Moving Pictures*), turning up the music and smiling, and—self-referentially—drumming and beating at the hearts of an English winter and an African village (Peart's first book was about bicycling in Africa). "The Larger Bowl" (the fourth song) begins with a heavy introduction that is recalled later and also previews the heavier style of the song's chorus. However, the song's verses use Alex Lifeson's layered, "heavy acoustic" guitars and Geddy Lee's vocals in a moderate, high-baritone range. The song discusses the hardened, difficult sociological and geopolitical discrepancies that exist between "golden ones" (the more fortunate among us) versus those who are "scarred from birth" (the poor, the third world, and so on). The guitar solo also expresses the song's heavy versus acoustic disparity by mostly featuring Lifeson's poignant, bluesy electric playing over his own acoustic accompaniment.

"The Larger Bowl" merges gaplessly into the album's fifth song, "Spindrift," which applies a somewhat-psychedelic, stylistically heavy style within an analogy based on the meteorological condition of crashing waves (and sand) meeting strong winds. The idea is that one's "devil wind," whipped-up mental state would also be precariously balanced. The song's main, angular, instrumental gesture provides a parallel by descending through a small then large interval, followed by an opposite, ascending motion. In a relationship, though, responding to someone else's words could easily compromise such an already-edgy scenario to the breaking point: "What am I supposed to say? Where are the words to answer you when you talk that way?" So, the recurring music underlying that idea ascends through a narrower set of very small intervals—while also broadening in texture and volume—in a manner that significantly increases the tension. Another part of the song, using relatively happy-sounding music, proposes the possibility of a wave coming in that would allow the protagonist to be carried a little closer to the loved one. However, the song's main gesture returns for a lengthy restatement and fade-out, which suggests that the interaction of the "Spindrift" mental state, added tension, and closeness-enabling waves will continue as an ongoing process.

The band included several instrumentals on its first seventeen studio albums, but it never included more than one per album. "The Main Monkey Business" (the sixth song) is, however, the first of three instrumental pieces on *Snakes & Arrows*. The song mainly features electric guitar, bass, and drums, but all of those elements are considerably overdubbed and/or layered at times, and it also includes some quite frantic smaller-scale rhythms. On the other hand, its moderate/walking tempo and subtle synthesized elements, occasional wordless vocals, and acoustic guitar sometimes give the song a relatively laid-back feeling. The seventh song, "The Way the Wind Blows," begins subtly out of the preceding instrumental piece, with an isolated drum fill and then a quite blues-oriented, "wailing" opening. The song's verses feature complex, syncopated rhythms, and their lyrics have to do with extremism and intolerance, such as religion versus science and the environment. The main idea is that such attitudes actually come from the "Middle West" (e.g., the American Midwest) just as much as they do from the Middle East. The song's chorus, though, is more conciliatory and "soft," including acoustic guitars, overdubbed vocal harmonies, and the idea of living in the reality of the present and not being broken down by those who speak falsely. The song is followed by the album's second instrumental piece, "Hope," which is actually a solo, triple-beat (waltz-like) acoustic-guitar performance by Alex Lifeson. It somewhat picks up on the pleasant, conciliatory tone of the previous song's chorus. The compilation fund-raiser album, *Songs for Tibet: The Art of Peace* (2008), included a Grammy-nominated live version of "Hope."

The following three songs all fit stylistically somewhere between hard rock and soft rock, something like "ideological power ballads." In "Faithless" (ninth), Peart suggests that he doesn't have faith or belief in religion or even in the marketplace. He prefers to use his own moral compass, to keep his spirit level balanced, to resist the "shouting voices" and "fools and thieves," and to espouse hope and love. The theme of "hope" is thus instilled in the middle sections of the album. The song also includes a somewhat exotic-sounding, often-pitch-sliding string section, and Lee provides a higher-than-usual number of his own background vocals. "Bravest Face" somewhat responds to—or expands on— "Faithless" by exploring some complex things about our world. Similar to "The Larger Bowl," the song begins in a fairly heavy style, but its verses mainly use Lifeson's layered, "heavy acoustic" guitars. Verse 1 enthuses about the sunny viewpoint of the song "What a Wonderful World" (best known in the version from 1967 by Louis Armstrong), but it also points out that many people would hold a darker view of the world and thus not "get" such a positively spun song. In the verses, Lee occasionally "flips" his singing up to airy falsetto pitches that do not sound anything like his typical, piercing, high countertenor style of the 1970s and '80s or the more moderate high-baritone or tenor range he otherwise normally used in the 1990s and 2000s. The song's chorus is in a heavier style and succinctly points out further discrepancies, for example, "In the sweetest child, there's a vicious streak" and "In the strongest man, there's a child so weak." The album's eleventh song, "Good News First," also has relatively sparse (though electric) verses, a fairly heavy chorus, a certain degree of vocal-timbre experiments, a string section, and a bluesy (if short) guitar solo. Its lyrics have to do with the difficulties in communication of a couple trying to understand one another's confusing, changing worldviews.

The album's third instrumental piece, "Malignant Narcissism" (placed second last), is a frolicking, rhythmic, virtuosic hard rock piece that recalls Rush's slightly funky, fun instrumental works of the early 1980s and early 1990s: "YYZ," "Where's My Thing?" and "Leave That Thing Alone." Like those pieces, it was also nominated for a Grammy for Best Rock Instrumental Performance. The album's final song, "We Hold On," expands the theme of relationship stress from "Good News First" to include more abstract concepts that could also refer to anyone's stress about something that could lead to calling it quits, swallowing one's ambition, and so on. The song's chorus reflects the positive aesthetic, though, of someone who keeps going on and holding on. One of the variations of the chorus suggests that "there's a chance that we might not be so wrong." Indeed, Rush found quite a lot of vindication between 2007 and 2013 for its several decades of eccentric, progressive hard rock music and its provocative, individualist worldview.

FURTHER LIVE ALBUMS

In 2008, Rush released the double CD and DVD or Blu-ray *Snakes & Arrows Live*, recorded and filmed at the Ahoy Arena in 2007 in Rotterdam, the Netherlands. It features nine of its twenty-seven tracks taken from the band's recent studio album, although earlier Rush live albums (with the exception of the soundtrack CD of the 1985 *Grace under Pressure* tour video that was rereleased in 2006) had never covered so much of the band's most recent studio work. In 2009, the band released *Working Men*, a single-disc compilation album of well-known Rush songs performed live during their three major international tours of the 2000s. Then, the double CD and DVD or Blu-ray *Time Machine 2011: Live in Cleveland* was released in 2011 (from its 2010–2011 tour), on

Anthem in Canada, Roadrunner outside of Canada, and on Zoë Records (video only). The 2010–2011 tour also included the band's first complete performances of its highly successful 1981 album *Moving Pictures*. That was released separately as a special collector's item: *Moving Pictures: Live 2011*. Also in 2011, Rush appeared in satirical form on the TV show *South Park*, playing a progressive hard rock, fart-joke-laden, politically incorrect version of Elton John's soft rock ballad "Candle in the Wind."

CLOCKWORK ANGELS (2012)

In 2010, Rush released two new songs: "Caravan" and "BU2B" (which stands for "Brought Up to Believe"). The two songs then also appeared at the beginning of *Clockwork Angels* (2012), the band's nineteenth studio album of original music. The album was again coproduced by Nick Raskulinecz, recorded mostly at Toronto's Revolution Studio (in late 2011), but also at Nashville, Tennessee's Blackbird Studio (in the spring of 2010). *Clockwork Angels* is a progressive hard rock "concept album" that is also vaguely "steampunk," a science-fiction literary aesthetic that anachronistically places "futuristic" ideas (technology, architecture, mechanical computers, etc.) in the context of an earlier era—usually the nineteenth century. The album's story is not particularly coherent, compared to such concept albums as the Who's *Tommy* (1969), Pink Floyd's *The Wall* (1979), Marillion's *Misplaced Childhood* (1985), and Radiohead's *OK Computer* (1997). However, it does somewhat follow the story of a young man trying to come to terms with the confusing world around him: airships, imposed belief systems, mechanical beings, the distractions of mass entertainment, illusory love, hope of a better place, the possibility of other people having bad intentions, not regretting the past, and so on. Also, the "gapless" flow between many of the album's songs helps to solidify its continuous nature. Kevin J. Anderson, the *New York Times* best-selling American science-fiction author who had previously interacted with the lyrics of some of Rush's music (1984's *Grace under Pressure*), also expanded the album—based on Neil Peart's story and lyrics—into a novel: *Clockwork Angels: The Novel* (2012), with illustrations by longtime Rush album-cover artist Hugh Syme. In a related matter, Peart and Anderson also adapted it into a six-part graphic novel (part 1 released in March of 2014), with artwork by Nick Robles.

"Caravan"

The opening song, "Caravan," begins with sound effects of bells and engine sounds, which are then joined by quiet, gesturally inconclusive, descending instrumental patterns—themselves then doubled by a string section. The band then incorporates the introduction's paired, close-pitch patterns into the rhythmically decisive hard rock riff that introduces and underlies the first half of each of the song's verses. The lyrics come from the first-person "voice" of the album's protagonist, a young man watching a caravan of "steamliners" (airship transport vehicles) go by and imagining that they're taking him to the "distant dream of the city." The second half of each verse enacts the optimism by more frantically, rhythmically (almost funk-like) ascending—instead of methodically descending—through a more complex collection of close pitches. The song's chorus uses a different type of accompanying gesture (broken, "harp-like" chord pitches), and in it the young man tells us that he "can't stop thinking big." The song's second verse, about "breaking with the past," uses some quite experimental-sounding strings. The experimental strings also arguably give a sense of anachronistically adding something "new" (strings) to something "old" (progressive hard rock). In a sense, then, the song provides a steampunk, sci-fi update of Rush's 1982 song "Subdivisions."

"BU2B"

"BU2B" ("Brought Up to Believe") has the young man tell us about the belief system he has now rejected. The song starts somewhat psychedelically, with a weirdly masked introduction that hints at the "normal," full-volume, riff-based beginning that begins shortly thereafter. The forty-nine-second introduction gives the sense of a dream or confusion that then arrives at clarity. The lyrics don't mention a specific religion, but it seems quite likely that since "some will be rewarded" and the devil will "take the rest," that Peart is semiautobiographically referring to his own background in Protestant Christianity and projecting it into the album's larger story. He makes the idea somewhat more generic and "multi(anti)faith" than that, though, by also rejecting the idea that the universe has a plan and even that capitalism necessarily makes sense ("blind men in the market buying what we're told"). The unnaturalness of religion is underscored in the song's verses with the band's use of lurching, complex microrhythms that seem to be "additive" (e.g., 7/8 or 5/4), but are actually just very complex variations (including syncopations) of 4/4 or "common" time. The lyrics are similar to "Faithless" (from 2007's *Snakes & Arrows*), but with the addition of an imagined, manipulative deity, a "loving" (meant to be ironic) Watchmaker who "loves us all to death." The music of the chorus plays up the irony of the "loving" quality by being more normal sounding.

The Rest of *Clockwork Angels*

The title song, "Clockwork Angels" (third, 7:31 in duration), is a hard rock mini-epic that explains the existence in the album's narrative of mechanical false angels who supposedly serve the manipulative Watchmaker first mentioned in the previous song. The song's chorus has all living creatures duped by the compelling, synchronized, arm-spreading, singing "light goddesses" to "raise their hands as if to fly." Vocally experimental (electronically masked) sections of the song, though, hint at the true nature of the angels and their Watchmaker. In the song, Neil Peart postulates (Karl Marx–like) that even in sci-fi and cyberpunk, "religion is the opiate of the masses." "The Anarchist" (fourth) begins with a substantial, joyous-sounding instrumental introduction. The song's lyrics are then quite negative, about fending off the conscription attempts of well-off people who had themselves been duped by the Clockwork Angels and their Watchmaker. The song's music, though, is mostly very fast and positive, and the idea of rejecting expected social norms thus brings something of the relatively chaotic attitude of "punk" into Rush's peculiar version of "steampunk." The song's verse introductions recall the kind of sputtering, riff/texture interplay first used by Rush on some of its earliest music from 1975 to 1978. In the prechoruses, the protagonist's "silenced voice" is masked electronically. The same sections also feature a vaguely Middle Eastern–sounding string section. The song's chorus talks about internal lenses that paint the world black, buildups of anger, always being denied things, an "early promise that somehow died," and a "missing part" that traps you. Many people feel that way about how their lives have turned out.

The fifth song, "Carnies," flows directly from "The Anarchist," beginning with the brief appearance of carnival-like carousel music, combined with vaguely sinister mechanical sounds. The stylistically heavy, moderately fast song has to do with the types of entertainment provided by the Clockwork Angels in order to distract people from establishing their own goals and aspirations. The diversions include spinning lights and faces, demon music, iron wheels, bodies spinning in a clockwork dance, the smell of flint and steel, a wheel of fate, and a game of chance. "Halo Effect" begins with mysterious, soft, synthesizer sounds, which are then quickly replaced by a gentle, acoustic guitar (and, gradually, drums and bass) and mellow vocals. The lyrics explain how the story's protagonist had repeatedly become entranced with his delusional, illusion-projecting ideals of others (presumably meaning members of the opposite sex), instead of with real people. "Seven Cities of Gold" (the album's seventh song) at first features a bass-driven, fairly funky instrumental introduction. The song mainly explores a sociological parallel to "Halo Effect," this time about the "splendid mirage" or hallucination of places and things (i.e., the golden cities of the song's title) that have fired his imagination. The reality of wandering through canyons and deserts, experiencing desolation and cold, and being parched and sunblind is relieved by the promise—even if it's false—of a much better place. Similarly, the song's music remains active and positive throughout.

"The Wreckers" (eighth), a comparatively soft rock song, covers the idea of having to be wary of other people's intentions. It suggests that even if you move on from your unpleasant past, such as in a ship, future people might make things miserable for you once again. Breakers, ghostly lights, and helpful sounds might beckon you to the shoreline, but the people there ("the wreckers") actually just want to swarm and pillage the vessel that you thought would be your salvation. Sometimes the actual truth is the opposite of what you expected, a miracle is "too good to be true," and "the target is you." The irony of that sentiment is heightened by the use of a pleasant-sounding string section throughout much of the song. "Headlong Flight" (ninth) is a fast, active "progressive hard rock" song, including widely varying textures, virtuosic instrumental elements, jazzy extended chords, and even one section featuring strange/speech-based vocal effects. The lyrics have to do with not re-gretting the past—whether bad ("dark") or good ("bright")—and with wishing to live through the same things again. The song's chorus uses the steampunk analogy of working in a big machine ("stoking fire"), steering an airship across the stars, and learning to fight, love, and steal. Thus, the song arguably transforms Neil Peart's reserved, earlier senti-ments about fame in Rush's 1981 song "Limelight" into an older, wiser point of view. The song is arguably closer in style to "classic Rush" (i.e., 1975–1984) than anything else the band had done over the previous several decades.

"BU2B2"—a short, gloomy, electronic then strings-based variation of the album's second song—reminds us that "faith has failed me" and that "optimism has abandoned me." However, even though things may have gone from bad to worse, the song nonetheless manages to suggest that love, laughter, and life are still possible. "Wish Them Well" (the album's second-last song) returns to a relatively mainstream, hard rock style and lyrically spins a positive idea about abandoning grudges and just walking away from people who hold them against you. The album's final song, "The Garden," is a beautiful, texturally rich ballad unlike anything else Rush has ever done. It concerns the idea of reaching a pleasant state of happiness, fulfillment, and love, measuring the value of your life like a garden that you need to nurture and respect. The song also recalls the album's idea of a Watchmaker, but he "keeps to his schemes" and just causes the hours to tick away.

Rush embarked on another major tour in 2012–2013, and in 2013 *Clockwork Angels* won the Juno Award for Rock Album of the Year. Due to orchestral strings sometimes being used on the band's two most recent albums, a "punk"-like, very nonclassical string section toured with the band and joined in on a number of its newer—and occasional older—songs. Until 2012, in live performances Rush had always trig-gered its earlier occasional uses of nonband elements (orchestral instru-ments, a choir, keyboard parts originally played or programmed by re-cording studio associates, etc.) from recorded samples. The tour was documented in 2013, with Rush's release of the double CD and video *Clockwork Angels Tour*, which was recorded in 2012 in the United States at large arenas in Phoenix, Dallas, and San Antonio.

THE ROCK AND ROLL HALL OF FAME (2013)

After Rush first became eligible for induction into the U.S.-based Rock and Roll Hall of Fame, in 1999, *Rolling Stone* senior editor and Hall of Fame adviser David Wild responded to those wishing for it:

> It ain't ever going to happen. Regardless of their success, Rush has never achieved critical acclaim and no one will ever vote for them. Apart from "Tom Sawyer," most of their music gives me a headache.

In the subsequent dozen or so years, the decision makers at the Hall of Fame consistently did not nominate Rush. The annual "snub" infuriated the band's fans, especially given that a number of inductees in the 2000s included individual group members from the 1950s that very few people would even know by name. The "disconnect" vis-à-vis Rush between rock critics and music fans then came to a head in 2012, when the Hall of Fame first allowed public, Internet, "crowd-sourced" voting. Rush became one of the eight inductees for 2013, despite never having been earlier nominated by the popular music critical establishment.

Rush's induction into the Rock and Roll Hall of Fame derived from a combination of intense voting by the band's fans (including musicians, people who run Rush tribute websites, and bloggers) and a younger generation of rock critics impressed by the band's longevity, skills as musicians, and unusual vision. At the ceremony at the Staples Center in Los Angeles, Rush was inducted by the popular U.S. rock band Foo Fighters, who joined them in performing. The band's moment of acceptance included a very committed Alex Lifeson speaking nothing but "Blah, blah, blah" in a highly varied, often mock-emotional manner for several minutes. After fourteen years of rock critics saying that Rush would never, ever be inducted, there just weren't any actual words that would suffice for mocking such things.

CONCLUSION

"In the Fullness of Time"

After experiencing Rush—and hopefully listening to some of its music—you may not actually "like" the band. However, that has not been the point of this book. Instead, the point was for you to try to understand the music and context of a band about which you may not have known much—if anything. The band has been very influential, with hundreds of thousands of musicians and millions of others interested in at least some of its music. The range of Rush cover songs is quite indicative of the band's influence on other musicians, including such highly diverse areas as progressive hard rock, death metal, electronica, classical strings, jazz piano, and world music. The band, though, by not being obvious (i.e., by usually avoiding Top 40 and other mainstream styles of music), by bringing various influences into what it was already doing (music, lyrics, business activities, etc.), and by constantly challenging itself to grow and change, also made sense to fans who applied similar approaches in their own lives. In addition to musicians, that also included information technologists, engineers, architects, entrepreneurs, writers, non-music intellectuals, and many other types of people.

Rush has always been highly regarded by musician-fans and related magazines, such as *Bass Player*, *Guitar for the Practicing Musician*, and *Modern Drummer*. However, most general-interest music and cultural magazines, perhaps especially *Rolling Stone* (until 2012, anyhow), often considerably downplayed the band's accomplishments. The band became known mainly through its album-oriented rock and live touring. Despite what "alternative" meant starting in the early 1990s (indie music, grunge, etc.), Rush's uncompromising approach to its music and career means that it has actually always produced a variation of that idea. Rush pursued an adaptive/evolutionary and individualist approach to music making that resonated for others of the "post-counterculture," instead of the reactive/revolutionary and typically more political approach favored by most major rock critics of the 1970s, '80s, and '90s. In the 2000s, rock critics (and many others) finally caught up to what Rush had been doing all along.

Rush has won numerous awards in its native Canada. From 1975 to 2013, the band won nine Juno Awards (the "Canadian Grammy"), plus several additional ones for album designs by Hugh Syme. In addition, in 1979, the government of Canada named the band "Ambassadors of Music"; in 1990 Rush won the Toronto Music Awards Mayor's Award; in 1992 SOCAN's Harold Moon songwriting award; in 1993 the Toronto Arts Award; in 1994 a place in the Canadian Music Hall of Fame; in 1996 memberships in the Order of Canada (the nation's highest civic honor); in 1999 a star on Canada's Walk of Fame; in 2003 a place in Canada's Music Industry Hall of Fame; in 2010 a place in the Canadian Songwriter Hall of Fame; in 2012 the Governor General's Performing Arts Award (for lifetime achievement); and in 2014 honorary Doctorate of Music degrees from Nipissing University in North Bay, Ontario. However, despite those many awards in Canada, the band is not mainly a Canadian phenomenon.

Almost all of its several dozen albums have been certified at gold and/or platinum levels in a number of countries (including the United States), and the band has sold over forty-five million copies of its various albums worldwide. It has also toured to perform for hundreds of thousands of fans in sixty or seventy concerts in at least several countries (always including the United States and Canada) for at least five months of nearly every year from 1976 to 2013. Rush is thus arguably one of the world's most successful "cult bands." Also, between 1981 and 2011, the band was nominated for seven Grammy Awards. Then, from 2008 to 2014 it engaged quite actively with mainstream U.S. media. For the first time in the band's thirty-eight-year professional career, even *Rolling Stone* featured Rush in a 2012 cover story. It covered the band's new concept album, *Clockwork Angels*, but also the "snub" of the band perennially (until 2013) being bypassed for the U.S.-based Rock and Roll Hall of Fame. The moral of the story is this: when actual music fans get to participate in things such as awards nominations and when social media and grassroots movements tip momentum in directions other than those vetted by the critical establishment, artists such as Rush do get inducted into places like the Rock and Roll Hall of Fame.

SELECTED READING

Anderson, Kevin J. *Clockwork Angels: The Novel*. From a Story and Lyrics by Neil Peart. Toronto: ECW Press, 2012.

Armbruster, Greg. "Geddy Lee of Rush." *Keyboard*, September 1984, 56–65.

Banasiewicz, Bill. *Rush: Visions —the Official Biography*. London: Omnibus, 1988.

Berti, Jim, and Durrell Bowman, eds. *Rush and Philosophy: Heart and Mind United*. Chicago: Open Court, 2011.

Bowman, Durrell. "'Let Them All Make Their Own Music': Individualism, Rush, and the Progressive/Hard Rock Alloy, 1976–77." In *Progressive Rock Reconsidered*, edited by Kevin Holm-Hudson. New York: Routledge, 2002.

———. "Permanent Change: Rush, Musicians' Rock, and the Progressive Post-Counterculture." Ph.D. diss., University of California, Los Angeles, 2003.

"Counterparts." *Canadian Musician* 16.1 (1994): 37.

Counterparts. Tour booklet, 1993–1994.

Dome, Malcolm. "Interview with Neil Peart." *Metal Hammer*, April 25, 1988.

"The Drummer Sounds Off." *Rush Backstage Club* newsletter, March 1990.

Fish, Scott K. "Interview with Neil Peart." *Modern Drummer*, January 1986.

Foster, Richard S. "A Nice Morning Drive." *Road & Track*, November 1973, 148–50.

Garofalo, Reebee. *Rockin' Out: Popular Music in the USA*. Boston: Allyn & Bacon, 1997.

"Geddy Lee/Rush." *Canadian Musician*, May 1981, 34–35.

Gehret, Ula. "To Be Totally Obsessed—That's the Only Way." *Aquarian Weekly*, March 9, 1994.

Hamilton, Peter. "The Whole Is Greater Than the Sum of Its Parts." *Canadian Musician* 16.1 (1994): 36–39.

In the Studio with Redbeard. Show #28, week of January 2, 1989. Radio show.

"Interview with Alex Lifeson." *Guitar Player*, August 1988.

"Interview with Geddy Lee." *Melody Maker*, February 11, 1978, 14.

Johnson, Howard. "A Farewell to Bings." *Raw* (135), October 27/November 27, 1993.

Kordosh, J. " Rush: But Why Are They in Such a Hurry?" *Creem*, June 1981, 62 .

Krewen, Nick. "Rush: Presto Change-o." *Canadian Musician* 12.2 (April 1990): 37.

———. "Surviving with Rush: Drummer-Lyricist Neil Peart Looks Forward." *Canadian Composer*, April 1986, 8.

Lifeson, Alex. "Rush *Grace under Pressure*." As told to Jas Obrecht. Playback: The Making of an Album, *Guitar Player*, August 1984, 44–51.

Makowski, Pete. "Adrenalin Rush." *Sounds*, December 18, 1982.

McDonald, Chris. *Rush and the Middle Class: Dreaming in Middletown*. Bloomington: Indiana University Press, 2009.

Miller, William F. "Neil Peart: In Search of the Right Feel." *Modern Drummer*, February 1994.

———. "Neil Peart/Rush." *Modern Drummer*, December 1989.

Moleski, Linda. "Production Opens 'Windows' for Rush: Rock Group's New Album 'Powered' by New Sound." *Billboard*, November 16, 1985, 49.

Mulhern, Tom. "Geddy Lee of Rush, Rock's Leading Bassist." *Guitar Player*, April 1986, 86.

Myers, Paul. "Rush Put Themselves to the 'Test.'" *Canadian Musician* 6 (Dec. 1996): 34–39.

Peart, Neil. *Far and Away: A Prize Every Time*. Toronto: ECW Press, 2011.

———. *Ghost Rider: Travels on the Healing Road*. Toronto: ECW Press, 2002.

———. *The Masked Rider: Cycling in West Africa*. East Lawrencetown, NS: Pottersfield Press, 1996.

———. *Roadshow: Landscape with Drums; A Concert Tour by Motorcycle*. Burlington, Mass.: Rounder Books, 2007.

———. *Traveling Music: The Soundtrack to My Life and Times*. Toronto: ECW Press, 2004.

Pollock, Bruce. "The Songwriting Interview: Neil Peart." *Guitar for the Practicing Musician*, October 1986.

Popoff, Martin. *Contents under Pressure: 30 Years of Rush at Home and Away*. Toronto: ECW Press, 2004.

———. *Rush: The Illustrated History*. Minneapolis, Minn.: Voyageur Press, 2013.

"Profile: Alex Lifeson—Rush Strips Down." *Guitar Player*, December 1993, 21–22.

Rand, Ayn. "Apollo 11." *Objectivist* 8.9 (September 1969): 6–12.

Stern, Perry. "Rush: Baroque Cosmologies in Their Past, the Boys Focus on 'the Perfect Song.'" *Canadian Musician* 7.6 (1985).

Test for Echo radio premiere broadcast, Chicago, WKSC-FM, September 5, 1996.

Testa, Bart. Review of *2112*. *Crawdaddy*, December 1976, 73.

Tolleson, Robin. "Bass Is Still the Key." *Bass Player*, November/December 1988.

Weinstein, Deena. *Heavy Metal: A Cultural Sociology*. New York: Lexington Books, 1991.

Welch, Chris. Review of *All the World's a Stage*. *Melody Maker*, July 23, 1977, 38.

Widders-Ellis, Andy. "Alex Lifeson—Rush Strips Down." *Guitar Player*, December 1993, 21–22.

———. "Rush Redefined." *Guitar Player*, November 1991, 33–38.

SELECTED LISTENING

STUDIO ALBUMS

Rush released March 1, 1974, Moon Records (rereleased a few months later by Mercury Records).

Fly by Night released February 15, 1975, Mercury Records.

Caress of Steel released September 24, 1975, Mercury Records.

2112 released April 1, 1976, Mercury Records.

A Farewell to Kings released September 1, 1977, Mercury and Anthem Records.

Hemispheres released October 29, 1978, Mercury and Anthem Records.

Permanent Waves released January 1, 1980, Mercury and Anthem Records.

Moving Pictures released February 12, 1981, Mercury and Anthem Records.

Signals released September 9, 1982, Mercury and Anthem Records.

Grace under Pressure released April 12, 1984, Mercury and Anthem Records.

Power Windows released October 29, 1985, Mercury and Anthem Records.

Hold Your Fire released September 8, 1987, Mercury and Anthem Records.

Presto released November 21, 1989, Atlantic and Anthem Records.

Roll the Bones released September 3, 1991, Atlantic and Anthem Records.

Counterparts released October 19, 1993, Atlantic and Anthem Records.

Test for Echo released September 10, 1996, Atlantic and Anthem Records.

Vapor Trails released May 14, 2002, Atlantic and Anthem Records.

Feedback (tribute EP) released June 29, 2004, Atlantic and Anthem Records.

Snakes & Arrows released May 1, 2007, Atlantic and Anthem Records.

Clockwork Angels released June 12, 2012, Roadrunner and Anthem Records.

LIVE ALBUMS (SOME INCLUDING VIDEOS)

All the World's a Stage released September 29, 1976, Mercury Records.

Exit . . . Stage Left released October 29, 1981, Mercury and Anthem Records.

A Show of Hands released January 10, 1989, Mercury and Anthem Records.

Different Stages released November 19, 1998, Atlantic and Anthem Records.

Rush in Rio released October 21, 2003, Atlantic and Anthem Records.

R30: 30th Anniversary World Tour released November 22, 2005, Atlantic and Anthem Records.

Snakes & Arrows Live released April 15, 2008, Atlantic and Anthem Records.

Grace Under Pressure Tour released August 11, 2009 (recorded in 1984), Mercury and Anthem Records.

Time Machine 2011: Live in Cleveland released November 8, 2011, Roadrunner and Anthem Records.

Clockwork Angels Tour released November 19, 2013, Roadrunner and Anthem Records.

INDEX

ABOUT THE AUTHOR

Durrell Bowman culturally interprets music, and he has written studies of rock music and film and television music. He holds degrees from the University of Waterloo and the University of Toronto, as well as a Ph.D. in musicology from the University of California, Los Angeles (UCLA).

Dr. Bowman coedited *Rush and Philosophy: Heart and Mind United* (2011), authoring three of its chapters. He has also done work on an additional book project: *Be Sharp: "The Simpsons" and Music*. In addition, he has published other book chapters and journal articles, delivered conference papers and invited talks, prepared interviews, and written program notes, reference entries, and book and media reviews. As a visiting and part-time instructor, he developed and taught over twenty different university courses at seven institutions.

He occasionally composes music and frequently performs as a choral singer, pianist, song leader, and soloist. He is an amateur photographer and genealogist.

Dr. Bowman returned to school in 2009–2010 to study software development. In a related paid internship, he developed the American Musicological Society's new, web-based version of *Doctoral Dissertations in Musicology* and created web-based program notes for the Bowdoin International Music Festival. Since then, he independently created OurMus.Net (a collaborative community website for music history and culture), produced web-based music history instructional videos, and has developed and/or administered additional websites, including the one for the Grand Philharmonic Choir.

More information about Durrell Bowman can be found at http://durrellbowman.com/.